From Peter
To Chris, July 2021

THE
RENAISSANCE

THE
RENAISSANCE

THE CULTURAL REBIRTH
OF EUROPE

John D. Wright

amber
BOOKS

Published by
Amber Books Ltd
United House
North Road
London
N7 9DP
United Kingdom
www.amberbooks.co.uk
Instagram: amberbooksltd
Facebook: www.facebook.com/amberbooks
Twitter: @amberbooks

ISBN: 978-1-78274-904-2

Project Editor: Sarah Uttridge
Designer: Jerry Williams
Picture Research: Terry Forshaw

Printed in China

CONTENTS

CHAPTER 1

Origins

Some historians dispute both the term 'Renaissance' and its dates, generally set between the fourteenth and sixteenth centuries. They agree, however, that the powerful Italian city states, led by Florence, were growing rich on Mediterranean trade and used their wealth to promote this flowering of intellectual and artistic ideas.

THE TERM 'Renaissance', which is French for 'rebirth', was a convenient way to describe the new interests in culture, science and exploration that began around the fourteenth century. Most scholars today prefer to regard this activity as a renewed interest in classical knowledge, rather than a modern leap forward. Progress did occur with the new awareness of how much knowledge and wisdom had been lost during the stagnant Middle Ages. Italian humanists emphasized those dark years of feudalism to show they were living in a new age, with a new spirit driven by the rediscovery and renewal of the ancient Greek and Roman cultures.

The first indications of the Renaissance occurred in the Italian arts in the 1300s at the close of the Gothic age. Known as the 'trecento' period, this new artistic awareness was halted in 1348 by the plague. In Florence alone, it reduced the population

OPPOSITE: *Dante Explaining the Divine Comedy* (1456), a fresco in Florence's Duomo by the Florentine painter Domenico di Michelino.

from 120,000 in 1348 to 50,000 three years later, and it also drove many artists from cultural centres in the city states. Despite such a devastating delay, the influential Italian poet Francesco Petrarca, known as Petrarch (1304–74) promoted the concept of regaining lost classical learning, and this idea evolved into the Renaissance. At the same time, the human values and introspection that motivated Petrarch's life spread the idea of 'humanism', a movement which also became a stimulus for cultural rebirth.

THE REDISCOVERY OF CLASSICAL CULTURE

BELOW: Constantinople fell in 1453 to the forces of Sultan Mehmet II after they destroyed the city's massive fifteenth-century walls.

The Renaissance began with efforts to study and surpass the lost cultures of ancient Greece and Rome, to promote a return to classical values and wisdom. Advocates in the fourteenth century regarded the writings of Aristotle, Cicero and other classical thinkers as a recovered reality, compared to the recorded ideas of medieval Christianity.

Rome began ruling the city states of Greece in 146 BC after its victory in the Battle of Corinth. The Greek world of ideas, such as in art and architecture, greatly influenced the Romans. When the Roman Empire in Western Europe fell in 476, Greece continued as the major strength of the Byzantine Empire, the eastern half of the Roman Empire. It protected the empire against invaders until Constantinople fell to the Ottoman Turks in 1453. This drove Byzantine scholars into Western Europe, which benefited from Arabic copies of ancient Greek texts. For example, the humanist Petrarch and others in Padua acquired Byzantine manuscripts of Homer's writings. The Byzantines had learned to make paper from the Arabs; a process they passed along to the Italians, who had developed a growing paper industry by the thirteenth century.

ABOVE: The poet and scholar, Petrarch, collected classical manuscripts for the humanistic inspiration that was the driving force for the Renaissance.

Much of this written culture had been lost or at least overlooked after Rome's fall. Romans who had studied and written classical Latin no longer made an effort as their educational system deteriorated, leaving the language in the hands of the church, whose texts had to be slowly copied by monastic scribes.

THE RISE OF HUMANISM

Humanism, also known as Renaissance humanism, was the driving force for this rebirth of classical knowledge. Its advocates wished to study and refine human potentialities, rather than rely only on rewards offered by the abstract teachings of Christian spirituality. They believed this could be accomplished by discovering and translating the works of ancient Greek and Roman thinkers in such fields as art, literature, philosophy, politics and history. Renaissance humanism would be a revival of the Roman concept of 'humanitas', an intellectual search for human virtue.

The Italian poet and great scholar Petrarch had the most influence in the development of the Renaissance. He lived around several Italian city states, including Florence, and developed a love for ancient authors. He studied classical Latin, which he used during his European travels to discover old manuscripts in monasteries and libraries, a quest that even unearthed letters written by the great Roman orator, politician and philosopher Cicero. At the same time, Petrarch had refined the sonnet and became the first modern Western poet to be crowned Poet Laureate of Rome in 1341.

KEY TO THEIR FREEDOM WAS THE WEAKENED AUTHORITY OF THE HOLY ROMAN EMPIRE AND THE PAPACY.

Despite his humanism, Petrarch had taken minor ecclesiastical orders in 1326 and believed classical writings contained a spiritual message. He felt the church should not be downplayed, believing God had placed mankind as the rational overseer of His creation.

ITALIAN CITY STATES

Independent city states were crucial to the birth and growth of the Renaissance. This collection of powerful cities evolved in the Middle Ages, and controlled their surrounding areas and sometimes other cities. Key to their freedom was the weakened authority of the Holy Roman Empire and the papacy, especially in northern city states such as Florence, Siena and Venice. The Catholic Church had control in the central cities such as Ferrara and Urbino. The independent northern cities tended to be self-governing republics and their citizens made their own laws, although real power was held by nobles and budding capitalists. They became rich by producing woollen cloth and other popular items for the growing Mediterranean trade and through banking, which was dominated by the powerful Medici family. This wealth led to patronage of the arts and great public projects, such as the construction of the cathedral of Milan.

Florence, driven by its energetic citizens and enormous wealth, initiated the Renaissance in the fourteenth century. This city state, which then had a population of some 95,000, was home to the Medici bankers and such cultural giants as

Leonardo da Vinci, Michelangelo, Dante and Galileo. Florence protected its citizens and its wealth by constructing towering walls between 1285 and 1340. The city was governed by an elite class drawn from guilds, and they elected the supreme magistrates who ruled Florence, although most of the real power lay with the city's wealthy bankers and businessmen.

Venice was unique among Italian city states, in that its independence would eventually last for 1000 years from the late seventh century to the late eighteenth century, making it the longest republic that has ever existed. This, and its ideal location for shipping, allowed the city to engage in extensive trade with

BELOW: Venice and the canals shown in 1338 when its fleet was all powerful. This image is in Oxford's Bodleian Library.

Europe as early as the Middle Ages, making it a natural centre for the commercial and artistic exchanges during the early Renaissance that it had adopted from Florence. Venice also provided ships for the Fourth Crusade, which set out to recapture Jerusalem for Christendom but instead looted Constantinople in 1204. The prominence of the Venetian fleet was secured by its defeat of Genoa's in a war that lasted from 1350 to 1381.

THE MEDICI

The Medici family, or House of Medici, became wealthy during the fourteenth century in Florence through banking and commerce. The powerful Medici dynasty was begun by Giovanni di Bicci de' Medici, whose elder son Cosimo the Elder (1389–1464) ruled Florence from 1434 until his death. He had ancient manuscripts collected for an impressive library where

MARCO POLO

PERHAPS THE BEST-KNOWN native Venetian was the explorer Marco Polo (*c*.1254–1324). His trips into China were actually made with his father and uncle, who were diamond merchants. In 1275 they arrived at the summer court of Kublai Khan, the Mongol ruler of China, who sent them on many missions around his country. The Polos stayed for 17 years, before arriving back in Venice in 1295. Marco then took part in a naval battle between Venice and Genoa, and was captured in 1298 by the Genoese and imprisoned. While there, his stories of his Chinese adventures were written down by a writer from Pisa and published in many languages. The popularity of these tales helped to spur the spirit of exploration that flourished in the Renaissance.

manuscripts by humanists and others were copied and disseminated. He attended lectures by Greek scholars and became a great admirer of Plato, even recreating Plato's Academy in his own villa. Cosimo and his sons were devoted patrons of the arts, enabling the Renaissance culture to flourish in Florence, which also became the birthplace of European culture. This patronage was intensified by Cosimo's grandson, Lorenzo the Magnificent (1449–92), who supported such renowned artists as Botticelli, Leonardo da Vinci and Michelangelo.

Members of the family became involved in banking in Florence, with the Medici Bank opening in 1397. They replaced the Bard and Peruzzi families, whose international financing was bankrupted in 1345 when England's King Edward III defaulted on his enormous debt. One of the innovations of Italian banking was its method of accountancy with double-entry bookkeeping and the use of Arabic numerals replacing Roman ones.

Since wool and cloth were the main Florentine products in the fourteenth century, the Medici Bank formed partnerships with companies making those successful exports. To avoid the Catholic Church's ban on usury, the bank hid interest on loans as other payments. The Tuscan term for this was *rischio*, from which the English word 'risk' is derived. By 1402, the bank had established a branch in Venice, the first of many in such cities as Milan, Geneva and London, making the Medici Bank the largest of its time. Florence itself became recognized as the leading centre of

ABOVE: Cosimo the Elder was the first Medici to rule Florence, making decisions from behind the scenes without ever holding office.

ABOVE: Florence's Uffizi Gallery has grown from Cosimo's small collection to become a famous museum, now visited by some 10,000 people a day.

money and banking when the city's golden florin coin, first minted in 1252, was distributed by trade throughout Europe.

The Medici family glorified its wealth and power by its patronage of Italy's best artists, commissioning them to construct and decorate large churches and create palazzos that covered acres in the city centres. In addition, they amassed personal collections of paintings that usually included their portraits. Cosimo I (1519–69) began a small museum of art in the Uffizi ('office') administration building he commissioned for the city in the sixteenth century, and this would grow to house the art collections of the grand dukes of Tuscany before it was opened to the public in 1769 as Florence's world-famous Uffizi Gallery.

THE *TRECENTO*

The *trecento* was an Italian term first used in the nineteenth century to describe the early Renaissance of the fourteenth century, the word being a shortening of *mille trecento* (or 1300). It lasted until 1400 and was a highly creative time, spanning Medieval Gothic art and that of the early Renaissance. The most influential art was produced by the Florentine Proto-Renaissance School led by Giotto di Bondone (1267–1337), who was famed for his figurative paintings, and the Sienese School led by Duccio de Buoninsegna (1255–1318), which created a modern version of Byzantine art known as International Gothic and was famed for its colourful religious paintings. Other important artists of the Pre-Renaissance were Simone Martini (1284–1344), who was known for his illuminated manuscripts and had been the pupil of either Giotto or Duccio, and the brothers Ambroglio Lorenzetti (1290–1352) and Pietro Lorenzetti (1280–1348). After their early interest in Florentine art, the brothers developed their own styles in Siena; Ambroglio specialized in perspectives and ornamentation, while Pietro is known for his realism and array of colours.

Impressive sculpture was also created during the *trecento*. In Pisa, outstanding work was done by Giovanni Pisano (1250–1314) and Andrea Pisano (1295–1348), who were not related. Giovanni's masterpiece, completed in 1301, was the pulpit of Pistoia Cathedral, on which he carved the expressive agony of figures in the Annunciation and Nativity. The English sculptor Henry Moore called him 'the first modern sculptor'. He greatly influenced the Pisa sculptors Andrea Pisano and

FROM DUNGEON TO DICTATOR

COSIMO THE ELDER WAS the wealthiest man in Europe, deriving profits from the Medici-owned bank that managed the papacy's finances and from the monopoly Pope Pius II had granted for mines that produced alum (metal salts) for Florence's textile industry. However, his power did not save him from a coup by the rival Albizzi family. When Cosimo was on holiday in 1431, a summons came indicting him for the crime of seeking to 'elevate himself higher than others'. He returned to be held in a tiny dungeon in the Palazzo Vecchio, Florence's government building. His death sentence was passed, but Cosimo bribed the Head of Justice to reduce this to banishment. While he spent a year in exile in Padua and Venice, the Medici family fixed the Florentine elections, taking control of the city's government. Cosimo returned in triumph and banished the Albizzi forever. With this done, he corrupted his way back to the top, assuming dictatorial powers behind the scenes for the rest of his life.

Giovanni di Balduccio (c.1290–1349), both of whom had worked in the Gothic style of art.

Trecento sculpture and architecture were closely related. Andrea Pisano carved three bronze doors for the baptistery of Florence Cathedral, completing them in 1336 under the watchful direction of Giotto, the cathedral's chief architect. In the following year, Giotto died, and Pisano succeeded him, going on to construct a *campanile* or bell tower adorned with carved reliefs and statues. His most renowned pupil was Andrea di Cione, who combined the talents of an artist, sculptor and architect.

BELOW: *Madonna and Child* (1310–15) was by the Florentine artist and architect Giotto who followed the new trend for naturalistic painting.

Few could read or write during this period, but some authors did make major contributions to Italian literature. Dante, Petrarch and Boccaccio stood above many minor writers and left valuable works that influenced future generations.

Dante's epic poem *The Divine Comedy* (*La Commedia*) was published in 1320. This powerful work created a humanistic view of a visionary world: Dante (1265–1321) wrote his own first-person journey through Hell, Purgatory and Paradise, and this personal account, written in the Tuscan vernacular, proved a major step for the Renaissance. It inspired the future work of artists from Botticelli to Salvador Dalí and the sculpture of Rodin. Petrarch developed the sonnet and became the most celebrated poet of his era, while Boccaccio (1313–75) popularized vernacular literature and is known for his masterpiece, the *Decameron*, an allegorical poem written from between 1348 and 1353 as a down-to-earth look at the sadness and joys of life. His vernacular prose would influence writers throughout

Europe, including England's Geoffrey Chaucer. Boccaccio first met Petrarch in 1350 in Florence, and the two worked together to develop the humanism of the Renaissance.

THE FOUR CIONE BROTHERS

Although Andrea di Cione (1308–68), also called Orcagna, was universally recognized as a brilliant painter, sculptor and architect, he often collaborated with his three brothers, Jacopo, Nardo and Matteo. All were well versed in the same arts and Orcagna's work was sometimes attributed to Nardo, his oldest brother. Jacopo, the youngest, often completed the unfinished works of the others. Among his own art is the altarpiece for the Church of San Lorenzo in Florence.

FEW COULD READ OR WRITE DURING THIS PERIOD, BUT SOME DID MAKE MAJOR CONTRIBUTIONS TO ITALIAN LITERATURE.

Orcagna's most notable sculpture was a marble tabernacle commissioned by the Brotherhood of Orsanmichele and paid for from offerings to the Virgin during the plague of 1348. His most admired paintings in Florence included *Vision of St Bernard* in the Academy of Florence and *Coronation of the Virgin* in the church of San Pier Maggiori. In that same church, Jacopo collaborated with Niccoló di Pietro Gerinion the 12-panel altarpiece in 1370, some of which is now in London's National Gallery. Following the death of Matteo, Jacopo completed his unfinished marble sculptures in Florence Cathedral.

DANTE ALIGHIERI

Dante was born in Florence into a politically active family and, early on, he hoped to become a pharmacist. In 1285 he entered into an arranged marriage to a family friend despite being in love with Beatrice Portinari, whom he would make the character of heavenly enlightenment in *The Divine Comedy*. She died in 1290 and Dante recounted his lost love in his first poem, *The New Life*. He turned to politics, holding key public offices. He supported the rights of the monarchy in general, as he wrote in his *De Monarchy* and this brought him into conflict with Florence's rulers, who supported the pope. In 1302, at

ABOVE: *Dante and Petrarch* (*c.*1430) is a humanist image by Giovanni dal Ponte from Florence who helped develop early Renaissance painting.

the age of 37, Dante was exiled from his beloved city for the rest of his life, which lasted for two more decades. During this time he wrote various poems and theoretical essays on a wide range of subjects, such as philosophy and politics. More importantly, he wrote his epic masterpiece, *The Divine Comedy*, completing it in Ravenna a year before his death there.

GIOTTO DI BONDONE

Giotto has been called the first great Italian master and the father of European painting. He was supposedly a pupil of Cimabue at the end of the thirteenth century and realized that painter's unfulfilled desire to loosen up the stylized form of medieval painting. Giotto added realism and passion to human figures, his most popular subjects, giving them new humanity. He also added perspective to his scenes and was perhaps the first painter to use it. Among his renowned paintings is *The Nativity*, part of his fresco cycle that was painted around 1305 in the Scrovengi Chapel at Padua. At about this time, he also painted several works in Rome, including the *Navicello* (or *Christ Walking on the Water*) over the entrance to St Peter's.

Giotto was an innovator who rejected the stilted art of the Middle Ages and created a new standard of reality that would be adapted by later Renaissance artists like Michelangelo. Such was his fame, he was mentioned during his lifetime by Dante in *The Divine Comedy*.

THE RENAISSANCE SPREADS

Extending the Italian Renaissance to wider Europe required good communications, and this came about when Germany's Johannes Gutenberg invented the printing press and introduced it in 1440,

A VISIT TO HELL

IN *THE DIVINE COMEDY*, Dante is conveyed to hell by the Greek mythological figure Charon past the famous sign that warns: 'Abandon hope all ye who enter here'. His tour guide is the great Roman poet Virgil, who shows him horrific torture scenes. Satan himself appears, with three mouths constantly devouring Judas, Brutus and Cassius. In placing the betrayer of Christ next to those who assassinated Julius Caesar, Dante emphasized the importance of Christ and Caesar as representatives of the spiritual and humanistic worlds. Other victims are Dante's contemporaries, including politicians who had taken bribes now stuck eternally in hot pitch to recall their sticky fingers. Another gruesome encounter is with Pisa's Count Ugolino, seen gnawing on the skull of Archbishop Ruggieri, who in 1289 had sealed the count with his two sons and two grandsons in a tower and let them starve to death.

The devil sits in the centre of tortured souls in this depiction of Dante's Inferno in *The Divine Comedy*.

replacing wooden blocks with movable type. The wisdom of the past could then be widely circulated since books were mass produced on presses throughout Western Europe. More than 20 million volumes were printed by 1500 and this rose to 200 million by 1600. Gutenberg's greatest accomplishment was the Gutenberg Bible, bringing that book into many hands outside the church. His invention also led to the first mass-produced newspapers. Germany's Johann Carolus printed an early newspaper in 1605 in Strasbourg, and its popularity inspired similar publications in Basel, Frankfurt and Berlin. England's first newspaper, the *Oxford Gazette*, was published in 1665 when London was ravaged by the plague; the first daily, the *Daily Courant*, appeared in London in 1702.

HANS HOLBEIN

HE WAS KNOWN AS Hans Holbein the Younger because his father was a successful artist. The son was born in Augsburg in Bavaria and migrated to Basel in Switzerland, but was soon attracted to the Italian Renaissance. He was influenced by the art of Albrecht Dürer and in 1515 met the Dutch humanist Desiderius Erasmus, who presented him with a copy of his *Praise of Folly*. Holbein went to England in 1526 seeking work, the first excellent painter schooled in the Italian Renaissance to spend time there. A Catholic, in 1527 he painted Sir Thomas More, England's

LEFT: Hans Holbein the Younger's self-portrait (*c*.1542-43) is in Florence's Uffizi Gallery.

Lord High Chancellor, who in 1534 stood up to Henry VIII, opposing his divorce and his split from Rome to head the Church of England. He returned to Switzerland that year but was horrified when Protestants smashed art and statues in Basel Cathedral. Holbein returned to England to paint portraits, including that of Thomas Cromwell. Eventually, in 1536, he painted the first of several portraits of Henry VIII, accurate works that displayed the detailed realism of Renaissance art.

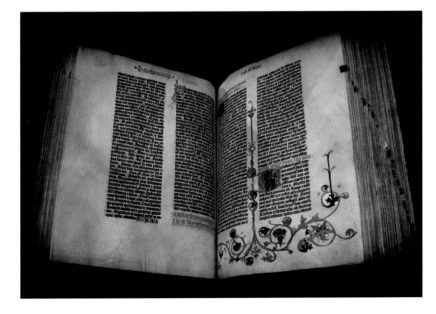

The Renaissance reached Europe in the fifteenth century. Western Europeans were attracted by the wealth and cultural vitality of the Italian cities, including many scholars, bankers and artists who would return home imbued with the ideas of the Renaissance. This took different forms according to local cultures but always promoted the humanistic look back at Greek and Roman wisdom. One who profited from the Italian Renaissance was Germany's Albrecht Dürer (1471–1528) from Nuremberg. His stay in Italy from 1505 to 1507 inspired his interests in human proportion and linear perspective. The intellectual ideas of humanism are reflected in his woodcuts and engravings that combine German influence with Italian style. Another who studied art in Italy was Pieter Bruegel the Elder (1525–69) from Flanders (now Belgium), who painted people as they lived, showing them working, having meals and at leisure.

EUROPEAN LITERATURE

European writers also profited from their Italian experiences. Miguel de Cervantes (c.1547–1616) was born near Madrid and went to Rome, where he became familiar with Renaissance literature and art. He also enlisted as a Spanish soldier in Naples and in 1575 was captured by Ottoman pirates and imprisoned in

Algiers for five years, being released by ransom in 1580. He returned to Madrid and combined his dramatic experiences and Renaissance outlook to write about real life, using the vernacular language. This resulted in his masterwork, *Don Quixote*, published in two parts in 1605 and 1615, and often regarded as the first modern novel.

Important thinkers in northern Europe advanced the Renaissance by the spread of their own books. Desiderius Erasmus (*c.*1466–1538), the Dutch humanist from Rotterdam, wrote a harsh criticism of the clergy and scholars in his *Praise of Folly*, published in 1509. Martin Luther (1483–1546), the German theologian who called Aristotle his teacher, was the key mover of the Protestant Reformation. England's Sir Thomas More (1478–1535) wrote *Utopia* in 1516, envisioning the ideal society where religious tolerance exists, both men and women are educated, and all politicians are honest. William Shakespeare (1564–1616), whose first collection of plays was published in 1623, highlighted the human condition by dramatizing problems that affected the lives of royalty and commoners.

As Europeans embraced the Renaissance spirit of being in charge of the natural world, they also made impressive advances in science and exploration. Among his many endeavours, the Florentine Leonardo da Vinci (1452–1519) made studies in anatomy, making dissections of some 30 corpses to observe how the human body worked and calling it 'man's instrumental figure'. This interest would later be followed by other Europeans, including Andreas Vesalius (1514–64) of Brussels, who completed his medical studies in Padua. In 1539 a judge there, knowing of Vesalius's interest in anatomy, offered him the bodies of executed criminals for dissection. His observations, recorded in his book *De humani corporis fabrica* (*One the Fabric of the Human Body*) in 1543, overturned centuries of medical misconceptions and transformed anatomy and surgery into practical fields based on observation.

Europeans also pursued the areas of exploration and science. Christopher Columbus, a native of Genoa, discovered the New World in 1492, and the Portuguese explorer Ferdinand Magellan (*c.*1480–1521) led the first voyage to circumnavigate the globe, which was completed in 1522, a year after he was killed by a local inhabitant on a Pacific island. This concept of man's mastery of the physical world was a Renaissance idea the Europeans would spread through the new lands they fought for and settled.

Another type of exploration of the solar system saw Leonardo da Vinci correctly identify earthshine on the moon's surface in 1510, while in 1543 the Polish astronomer Nicolaus Copernicus (1473–1543) published his shocking theory that the planets revolve around the sun.

DISCOVERY AND DEATH

SENT BY THE SPANISH king, Ferdinand Magellan left Spain in 1519 with five ships, aiming to find a westward route to the Spice Islands halfway around the globe and to gather their valuable products: cloves, black pepper, cinnamon and nutmeg. Within a month the small fleet had reached South America and in 1520 it sailed through the southern strait that would later bear Magellan's name. One ship had wrecked and one fled back towards Spain after a mutiny. Nevertheless, Magellan's men became the first Europeans to reach the Pacific Ocean, visiting the island of Cebu in the Philippines, where he converted its ruler to Christianity and agreed to fight his enemies on the island of Mactan. Thinking he could easily win with European weapons, Magellan led the attack from the front, despite warnings from his crew. A poison arrow soon found him and he died on 27 April 1521. One ship would continue westward and return to Spain on 8 September 1522, carrying 17 of the original 270 European explorers. The globe had now been circumnavigated for the first time.

CHAPTER 2

Art and Architecture

The Renaissance was first visible in the art world. Italian painters and sculptors could give their subjects new, realistic looks without writing down reasons for the changes. Most of the public was illiterate and didn't require intellectual arguments to appreciate these impressive visual works.

THERE WAS no assurance that art refinements made in the fourteenth century would continue. The Catholic Church was seldom pleased to see the spiritual appearance of saints replaced by more natural faces and by the removal of religious symbols surrounding them. Yet the church was not able to prevent the move toward realism and 'truer' images that employed new ideas such as the laws of perspective to create the illusion of depth and space. The subject matter of artworks also shifted. Artists inspired by humanism brought about a heightened interest in portraying non-religious figures, and they reintroduced the classic nude into their works. The new printing press was particularly important in spreading Renaissance art because it allowed copies of etchings, engravings and woodcuts to be seen throughout Europe and farther afield. In addition, artists personalized their work with self-portraits and

OPPOSITE: St Peter's Basilica was built between 1506 and 1626. Michelangelo designed the building but died before the dome was completed.

ABOVE: Francesca's *Flagellation of Christ* (late 1450s) used linear perspective. The artist unusually placed the main subject, Christ, in the background.

by adding images of themselves into their paintings. They even signed their names on works. Florence's Piero della Francesca was bold enough to pen his name in Latin at the feet of Jesus in his panel painting *The Flagellation of Christ*.

Sculpture was also changing, with its creators looking back at classical statues for inspiration but adding a new sense of reality, energy and movement to their works. Donatello added an expression of agony to his *St Mary Magdalene*, while Michelangelo and later Giambologna, a Flemish sculptor based in Italy, gave their subjects a sense of flowing motion.

Architects also sought to reinvent the great structures of the Roman Empire. They made countless visits to Rome and Athens, taking notes as they sketched the monuments of the Colosseum, the Triumphal Arch of Constantine, the Roman Forum, the Pantheon, the Theatre of Marcellus and other classical remains. This revived interest could be seen in the construction of St Peter's Basilica in Rome and later in the spread of triumphal arches, such as Arc de Triomphe in Paris and London's Wellington Arch, both built in the nineteenth century during a period of neo-classical revival. Details of ancient Greece's classical Doric, Ionic and Corinthian columns were widely reproduced and adapted for buildings around the world. Important examples in England include the British Museum and Blenheim Palace, while in America these features were heavily used in important public buildings, for example in Washington, DC on the US Capitol Building, the Supreme Court Building and the Lincoln Memorial. Columns also became a familiar front on many private homes in southern states and continue to be used for modern houses.

NEW PERSPECTIVES

Filippo Brunelleschi (1377–1446), a Florentine architect and engineer, was the first to use linear perspective in 1415. This illusion of depth, having parallel lines converge on a distant vanishing point with subjects becoming smaller with distance, brought an astonishing reality to the previous art of flat images. Some art historians believe this could have been a revival of the lost technique possibly used in ancient Greek and Roman art.

Brunelleschi was trained as a goldsmith and sculptor. He rediscovered the laws of linear perspective between 1410 and 1415 and first used the technique by painting the streets and buildings of Florence on two panels that have been lost. His rules for this were first written down by Leon Battista Alberti (1404–72), a humanist architect who was an associate of Brunelleschi's. Alberti's book *On Painting*, dedicated to Brunelleschi, was published in 1435 and revolutionized Italian art with its knowledge on how to organize space and depth to create a three-dimensional image. The elements of perspective continued to be investigated by such artists as Piero della Francesca, who wrote *On Perspective in Painting* between 1474 and 1482 and demonstrated the

BELOW: Brunelleschi statue (*c.*1838) by Luigi Pampaloni faces Florence's Duomo and shows the architect looking at the magnificent dome he completed.

technique in his own art, such as his fresco painting *The Legend of the True Cross*, completed in 1466 for the church of San Francesco in Arezzo. Others who mastered perspective included the sculptor Donatello and the artist Masaccio from Florence, the genius Leonardo da Vinci and Germany's humanist artist Albrecht Dürer.

After losing a competition in 1401 to Lorenzo Ghiberti to create seven gilded panels for the Florence Baptistery, Brunelleschi concentrated on architecture and in 1418 defeated Ghiberti for the massive project of building a dome over Florence's Cathedral of Santa Maria del Fiore ('The Duomo'). The seeming impossibility of covering the building's wide apse had confounded architects for years, but Brunelleschi worked on the challenge from 1420 to 1436 and successfully erected the world's largest masonry dome. His other accomplishments included designing and building fortifications for Florence and other cities and the invention of hoisting machines for the dome construction.

Related to perspective is the technique of foreshortening, which creates a three-dimensional view of a particular object whose proportions are changed to reflect the imagined position of a viewer. In real life this causes a distortion, depending on the distance and angle; for example, when facing the feet of a prone man, a viewer would see the feet appear larger and his head smaller. Invented by the ancient Greeks, foreshortening was reintroduced and refined by Renaissance artists. Andrea Mantegna (1431–1506), who became court painter in Mantua, used it for a low-angled impact in his *Dead Christ*, painted about 1480. His mastery of *sotto in su* ('from below to above') was used to foreshorten figures on ceilings, like his fresco in the Camera degli Sposi (Bridal Chamber) in Mantua, in which a flat ceiling appears to have a circular

BELOW: This fifteenth-century manuscript by the humanist artist and architect Leon Battista Alberti demonstrates the mathematics of perspective and foreshortening.

opening to the sky where figures look down from a balustrade. This striking use of foreshortening on ceilings was embraced by Antonio Allegri, known as Correggio(1494–1534), the most famous painter of the school of Parma. Among his masterpieces is the fresco of the *Assumption of the Virgin* on the dome of Parma's cathedral, giving the illusion of the vault of heaven with figures in the clouds.

ABOVE: Brunelleschi's dome for Florence's Cathedral of Santa Maria del Fiore was a miracle of design. The building remains the city's tallest.

MASACCIO (1401–28)

Born near Florence as Tommaso di Ser Giovanni di Simone Cassai, the Florentine artist Masaccio has been called the most revolutionary painter and perhaps the best in the fifteenth-century Renaissance, known as the *Quattrocento* (1400) period. His nickname means 'clumsy' because the hard-working, absent-minded painter paid no attention to his appearance or hygiene.

Masaccio was influenced by his contemporaries; by Brunelleschi regarding perspective and proportion and by his friend Donatello, whose classical sculptural techniques, using monumental figures and emphasizing gestures and emotion, were applied by Masaccio to his paintings. About 1427, Masaccio completed a series of frescoes started but abandoned by Masolino de Panicale in the Brancacci Chapel of Florence's church of Santa Maria del Carmine. In this work in 1424, Masaccio pioneered perspective and its vanishing point, as well as a single light source, to create a three-dimensional, realistic look previously unknown. This influential work has been called 'the Sistine Chapel of the early Renaissance'.

Masaccio then produced his second masterpiece, *Trinity*, in 1427 in Florence's church of Santa Maria Novella. It was the first Renaissance painting to use a one-point perspective that fixes the viewer's position. That year he also began *The Resurrection of the Son of Theophilu* sin the Santa Maria del Carmine church.

BELOW: Massaccio did not complete some of the fresco series in the Brancacci Chapel, and they were finished by Filippino Lippi.

It was never finished and, at the age of 27, in Rome he died under mysterious circumstances, perhaps from the plague, although some believe he was poisoned by a jealous artist. Although he had only painted for six years, Masaccio would have a strong influence on Leonardo da Vinci, Michelangelo and Raphael.

THE COLOURISTS

The Renaissance saw artists change from using water-based tempura paints on murals and wooden panels to oil paints on canvas. The oil created a luminosity that added more realism to broader subjects. Venice became the centre of oil painting in the sixteenth century led by the amazing colour talents of Titian, Tintoretto and Paolo Veronese. Renaissance artists used colours from many natural sources, such as insects (carmine red), plants (indigo purple) and minerals (azurite). Some colours were expensive to produce; making the deep blue ultramarine paint required the semi-precious gemstone lapis lazuli, which could only be mined in what is now Afghanistan and was then crushed into a fine powder. This expensive colour was kept for special use, such as for the raiment of Christ or the drapery worn by the Virgin Mary. Different colours were also used to create a sense of perspective, such as showing the darker colour of a deeper sea and a lighter one of a more distant sky.

RENAISSANCE ARTISTS USED COLOURS FROM MANY NATURAL SOURCES, SUCH AS INSECTS, PLANTS AND MINERALS.

TITIAN (1480–1576)

Tiziano Vecellio, known today as Titian, was a brilliant and influential Venetian artist whose use of oil glazes was a revolutionary method of painting. He was born in a village north of Venice and studied under Giovanni Bellini, Venice's famous artist who had switched from tempura paint to oils. Titian developed a lifelong love of rich, vibrant colours and the effects of light and shade. Most artists avoided the expensive ultramarine blue in favour of cheaper blue pigments like azurite, which had a greenish tone. Ultramarine was considered more precious than gold, and even Michelangelo could not afford it.

Titian, however, insisted on pure ultramarine and had first choice from trading ships bringing it from the east to Venice. Its stunning use could be seen in his paintings, such as *Bacchus and Ariadne* (1520), where the spectacular blue sky covers nearly half the canvas. He sometimes used other blue pigments as an underpainting before applying ultramarine more sparingly.

Known for his loose brushstrokes, Titian was universally recognized as the leading painter of Venice after his celebrated *Assumption of the Virgin* was installed in 1518 above the high altar in the Frari Church in Venice. His reputation spread throughout Europe, and leaders in several countries eagerly sought him out to paint their portraits. Among them was Charles V, the Holy Roman Emperor. Titian became his court painter in 1533 and painted Charles on his horse, creating a standard for equestrian portraits. Other subjects included Pope Paul III, Queen Isabella of Portugal and King Philip II of Spain. In Titian's last two decades Philip became his main patron, for whom he painted six large mythological paintings collectively called the *poesie*. These were based on the epic poetry of Ovid's *Metamorphoses,* and two of his works feature the goddess Diana.

TINTORETTO (1518–94)

Jacopo Robusti nicknamed himself Tintoretto ('little cloth dyer') from his father's trade. After the death of Titian, he was one of Venice's leading artists, along with Veronese; Titian had greatly influenced Tintoretto, despite expelling him as his young apprentice in a fit of jealousy. Tintoretto sought to combine Titian's mastery of colour with Michelangelo's energetic works, producing many large-scale paintings with swift, bold brushstrokes and dramatic lighting. He carefully studied foreshortening, once hanging wax and clay figures inside a doll's house to sketch them from below. Critics have often been overwhelmed by his dramatic colours and strident brushwork.

One called him 'the world's most daring painter', and the American novelist Henry James wrote: 'No painter ever had such breadth and such depth'.

Tintoretto's breakthrough work was *The Miracle of the Slave*, completed in 1548 and showing muscular, active figures created with varied brushstrokes. The following year he painted an altarpiece for his own Venice parish church, San Marziale. *Saint Martial in Glory with Saints Peter and Paul* combined Michelangelo-style poses with Titian drapery. (The 500th anniversary of Tintoretto's birth was celebrated in this church in 2018 and 2019). He completed several commissions for the Doge's Palace, as well as an impressive cycle of paintings for Venice's religious brotherhood, the Scuola Grande di San Rocco.

At the age of 70 he painted his largest work, *Paradise*, for the main hall of the Doge's Palace. Measuring 22.6m (74ft) by 9.1m (30ft), the colourful and busy scene is thought to be the largest painting ever on canvas.

BELOW: Tintoretto's *Paradise* contains some 500 characters, including prophets, apostles and saints. The artist was about 70 when he painted this.

A RUTHLESS COMPETITOR

TINTORETTO'S PERSONAL REPUTATION DID not match that of his art. He was known as *il furioso* ('the angry') for his aggressive nature and speed of work. He offended fellow artists with his competitive nature, and often employed underhand methods, sometimes undercutting rival artists by offering his works at a low price or even for free. Neither was he above cheating to win against others. When the Scuola Grande di San Rocco asked artists to compete for a ceiling painting of Saint Roch, Tintoretto held back as others presented their sketches. He then pulled back a covering from the ceiling to reveal the painting he had already completed. When the others complained furiously, he donated the work as a gift and it was graciously accepted. He eventually covered the ceiling with his paintings.

THE GRAND MASTERS

The fifteenth and sixteenth centuries saw the rise of the giants of Renaissance art whose names remain familiar today. Leonardo da Vinci, Michelangelo, Raphael and Botticelli were leading lights, as were other immensely talented Italian painters including Titian, Masaccio, Bellini and Caravaggio, and other Europeans such as Spain's El Greco and Germany's Holbein and Dürer.

The era also saw the advent of the 'Renaissance man', a title used to describe a person achieving success in many disciplines, inspired by the new encouragement given to human achievement. This was embodied in the pronouncement by Leon Battista Alberti that: 'A man can do all things if he will'. Alberti himself was a painter, architect, poet, mathematician and scientist, among other skills. The two artists who obviously deserve such recognition are Leonardo – who was also a sculptor, writer, scientist, astronomer, inventor and musician among other accomplishments – and Michelangelo – a sculptor, architect, poet and engineer, to name a few of his interests. The Renaissance man also existed outside art; England's Isaac Newton knew physics, astronomy, theology, mathematics and other subjects.

LEONARDO DA VINCI (1452–1519)

Leonardo was born in the town of Vinci in Tuscany, an illegitimate child raised by his grandfather. He studied in Florence under the sculptor Andrea del Verrocchio, who also handled art commissions. By 1472 Leonardo had become a member of the Compagnia di San Luca, a brotherhood of Florentine artists. During the next decade, he painted and drew sketches that showed his interest in anatomy, engineering, military weapons and geometry. In 1482 he moved to Milan, after convincing the ruling Duke Ludovico Sforza that he was an expert in military engineering as well as a painter and sculptor. Living in Milan for 17 years, Leonardo completed six paintings, including a commission from a confraternity (religious brotherhood) for an altarpiece. Between 1483 and 1486, he painted *The Virgin of the Rocks*, but when the brotherhood offered too little for the work, Leonardo entered 10 years of

LEFT: Leonardo's self-portrait which he named *Man in Red Chalk* was painted in 1512 when the artist was 60 years old.

BELOW: Leonardo's famous fresco, *The Last Supper*, reflects his belief that a subject's thoughts were reflected by their expression, posture and gestures.

MONA LISA STOLEN

IN AUGUST 1911 THE work was stolen from a wall in the Louvre and was not recovered until December 1913. The thieves were three Italians led by a handyman, Vincenzo Peruggia, and the crime made *Mona Lisa* the most recognized and valued painting after newspapers carried its image around the world. The robbers had hidden in a closet overnight and walked out with the painting under a blanket. Sixty detectives worked on the case and even had Pablo Picasso as one of their suspects. Peruggia, who kept the painting in his Paris flat, ended the mystery by trying to sell it to an art dealer in Florence. He was arrested and imprisoned for eight months, after saying he had wanted to return the *Mona Lisa* to its native country.

RIGHT: Officials gathered around the stolen *Mona Lisa* on its return to Paris on 4 January 1914.

litigation and eventually sold it to someone else. In 1508 the brotherhood convinced him to paint the subject again and the result now hangs in London's National Gallery.

One of Leonardo's finest and most famous works is *The Last Supper* fresco painted between 1495 and 1498 for the refectory (dining hall) of the church of Santa Maria della Grazie in Milan. In the huge work, which is 4.6m (15ft) high and 8.8m (29ft) wide, the artist gives Christ and his disciples' different expressions and gestures to reflect what he called 'physical and spiritual motion'. The refectory suffered bombing during World War II, but the painting survived behind sandbags. It has been restored several times, due to Leonardo's unusual choice to paint with tempura and oil.

OPPOSITE: For his realistic *Mona Lisa*, Leonardo used a new three-quarter pose that was quickly copied by other artists.

After stays in Rome and Milan, he accepted an offer from the French king Francis Ito become the 'first painter and engineer' of his royal court in 1517.

He took with him *Mona Lisa*, an oil-on-wood portrait begun in 1503 that was supposedly of the wife of a Florentine merchant. He finished it there and, when Leonardo died in 1519, the king displayed the painting in a gallery at his Fontainebleau palace. In the early nineteenth century, it hung for several years in Napoleon's bedroom in the Tuileries, then went to its present home in Paris's Louvre Museum. (Today more than six million people view the *Mona Lisa*'s enigmatic smile each year, spending an average of 15 seconds in front of the painting, making it the museum's most popular exhibit.)

During his lifetime, Leonardo kept notebooks reflecting his many interests in art, anatomy, biology and engineering, especially flying machines such as his envisioned helicopter. The books are filled with diagrams, sketches and notes in left-handed 'mirror' writing, which moves from right to left. He also had the habit of carrying loose papers while outside to record his observations, and many of these are held in the British Museum.

MICHELANGELO BUONARROTI (1475–1564)

Michelangelo was born in the village of Caprese near Florence. He began an apprenticeship in painting in 1488 under Domenico Ghirlandaio, Florence's most respected painter, and then lived in the household of Lorenzo de' Medici, whose patronage let him train as a sculptor. In 1496, he went to Rome, where he earned fame the next year carving the *Pietà* (the name for any devotional statue), now in St Peter's Basilica. When another artist received credit for the work, he carved 'Michelangelo Buonarroti, Florence, made this' across the sash on the Virgin Mary's body.

He returned to Florence in 1501 to paint and sculpt his monumental marble *David*, finished in 1504 and placed in front of the Palazzo dei Priori (since renamed the Palazzo Vecchio) as a heroic symbol of the city. Standing just over 4m (14ft) high, *David* has a relaxed pose, seemingly confident and invincible, even before facing the fearsome warrior Goliath. It now stands inside the Accademia Gallery.

Michelangelo left many other projects unfinished after Pope Julius II called him back to Rome in 1505 to sculpt his tomb with 40 large statues. Michelangelo only finished a sculpture of Moses for it because the two men argued over the cost, so the

THE AWESOME PANOPLY OF SCENES QUICKLY EARNED HIM THE REPUTATION AS ITALY'S GREATEST LIVING ARTIST.

artist turned his efforts to painting the vault of the Sistine Chapel in the Vatican from 1508 to 1512. This masterpiece depicts Old Testament figures with glorious colours and energetic poses that twist and turn; these are especially dramatic in *The Creation of Adam*, showing God reaching out to touch fingertips with his first human. The Sistine Chapel's idealized bodies are examples of the stylized mannerism introduced by Michelangelo. The awesome panoply of scenes quickly earned him the reputation as Italy's greatest living artist.

Michelangelo began to spend more time on architecture, especially on the powerful Medici family's parish church of San Lorenzo. Here, from 1520 to 1534 he designed the Medici Chapel for tombs of that family, creating four large marble

LEFT: *The Creation of Adam* is the Sistine Chapel's most famous image in which Michelangelo painted a human-like portrait of God.

statues representing day and night on one and dawn and dusk on another. He also designed a library annexe to the church and at the same time devised new fortifications for Florence to defend against cannon fire.

In 1534, he left Florence to spend the remainder of his life in Rome and returned to fresco painting for Pope Paul III, creating *The Last Judgement* for the altar wall of the Sistine Chapel between 1537 and 1541. The long painting shows the intense agony and ecstasy of those condemned or saved as they rise from their graves. He also spent much time writing letters and poetry; some 300 poems have survived, many are sonnets and madrigals about the importance of love in reaching the divine. He also

BELOW: Michelangelo's paintings on the Sistine Chapel ceiling were finished in four years with the help of four assistants from Florence.

PAINFUL PAINTING

CONTRARY TO THE WIDESPREAD idea that Michelangelo painted the Sistine Chapel's ceiling on his back, he was standing up on a platform that he designed. It covered half the chapel and he moved it to the other side halfway through the project. He left a sketch showing himself standing and reaching up his right hand to paint. More evidence comes from poems he wrote about the experience. One translation by Saul Levine, a New York art historian, recounts the artist's agony: 'My belly's pushed by force beneath my chin... My beard toward heaven, I feel the back of my Brain upon my neck... My brush, above my face continually Makes it a splendid floor by dripping down. My loins have penetrated to my paunch... In front of me my skin is being stretched while it folds up behind and forms a knot, and I am bending like a Syrian bow.'

designed the dome for St Peter's, where he was head architect, but died in 1564, leaving others to carry out the construction of the impressive structure. His final paintings were frescoes for the Vatican's Pauline Chapel.

SANDRO BOTTICELLI (1445–1510)

Born Alessandrodi Mariano Filipeppi in Florence, he was nicknamed Botticelli (from *botticello*, meaning 'small wine cast'). He proved to be a witty and hyperactive child, leaving school to become an apprentice of a goldsmith and then of the artist Fra Filippo Lippi. By 1470, he had his own workshop, and two years later he joined Florence's confraternity of painters, the Compagnia di San Luca. The Medici family became his patrons and Botticelli spent most of his career on projects for them and their friends.

In 1481 the pope summoned him to Rome to decorate the walls of the Sistine Chapel, the only work he would accept outside Florence. His chapel frescoes were the *Life of Moses* and the *Temptation of Christ*, and he also painted papal portraits. Botticelli became known for his graceful Madonnas and mythological figures. The next year, he returned to Florence and between 1478 and 1490 he created his decorative masterpieces

ABOVE: For The Birth of Venus (*c.*1485), Botticelli took inspiration from classical statues of Venus, the goddess of love and beauty.

in the classical style: *Primavera*; *The Birth of Venus* (now in Florence's Uffizi Gallery); the *Adoration of the Magi* in 1475; and *Venus and Mars* in 1485.

Botticelli's art bore a different look in the 1490s, reflecting the turmoil caused by the plague, invasions and the expulsion of the Medicis from Florence. His paintings became more simple, having a greater religious intensity brought on by his devotion to the fanatical preaching of the Dominican friar Savonarola. The artist's anxiety about the uncertain future is seen in his *Mystic Nativity*, completed in 1500. In his last years, Botticelli became depressed, isolated and poor as patrons and buyers lost their enthusiasm for his paintings.

RAPHAEL (1483–1520)

Born Raffaello Santi da Urbino in the small hill town of Urbino in central Italy, Raphael was the son of Giovanni Santi, an artist, poet and courtier who taught him the basics of art. He died when the boy was 11, and Raphael continued to paint in his father's workshop. Aged 17 he moved to the city of Perugia to study for four years under the renowned artist Pietro Perugino and become a master painter. He also studied the styles and techniques of Leonardo and Michelangelo. From 1500 to 1508, Raphael painted in Florence and its region of Tuscany, being known especially for his portraits and devotional panels of Madonna and Child.

In 1508, when he was 25, Raphael was called to Rome by Pope Julius II to redecorate his living quarters, for which he painted magnificent narrative frescoes in the classical style that influenced future artists. One was his masterpiece, *The School of Athens*, a fresco painted on the library wall of the Vatican palace that shows ancient Greek philosophers like Socrates and Aristotle. In 1511 he made an oil painting of Pope Julius II sitting in a chair with a pensive expression, a portrait so lifelike it influenced subsequent portraits of popes. In 1513, he painted *The Sistine Madonna*, well known for the two cherubim (angels) at the bottom; figures that are still reproduced today on everything from stamps to t-shirts.

During this time, Raphael's reputation grew as a portraitist and painter of historical figures and events. In 1514 he was appointed the pope's chief architect and the architect for St Peter's, helping to design the building's basilica. Three years later, he began his largest painting on canvas, entitled *The Transfiguration*. He remained in Rome until his death at 37 in 1520; the date of his death, 6 April, was also the date of his birth. Until the end, he maintained a large workshop, with some 50 assistants and students. By then the High Renaissance master had proven to be more versatile than Michelangelo (who believed Raphael copied his works) and more productive than Leonardo.

Raphael was buried in Rome's Pantheon at his own request. The inscription on his

BELOW: *The Transfiguration by Raphael* (1517–20) was his last painting. It depicts Christ in glory between the prophets Moses and Elijah.

SFUMATO

SFUMATO IS A TECHNIQUE derived from the Italian word *sfumata*, meaning 'to tone down'. It is the technique of softening the transitions between colours without lines or borders, blurring the changes from light to dark areas. Those who mastered the soft shading included Raphael, Correggio, Piero di Cosimo and Leonardo da Vinci, who called it 'in the manner of smoke'. Leonardo learned *sfumato* under the Florentine artist Andrea del Verrocchio, who developed it. Leonardo used it to soften the face of *Mona Lisa* by applying many thin layers of paint with his fingers. Raphael's works in *sfumato* include *Madonna of the Meadow* (also called *Madonna Belvedere*), where the softness is evident in the Virgin Mary's face. This painting also used *chiaroscuro*, a technique to contrast the light and dark shades, seen in her clothing.

marble tomb reads in part: 'Behold his almost-breathing images, and you will easily see the alliance of nature and art… In his life, great mother nature feared defeat, and in his death she herself feared to die.'

THE NORTHERN RENAISSANCE

The Renaissance would have had less impact and life without its adaptation by artists living in regions north of the Italian peninsula. The ideas of humanism, personal betterment and the renewal of classical art appealed to these artists in the fifteenth century, many of whom spent time in Italy and returned to make cities like London, Paris, Nuremberg and Antwerp into centres of humanistic art and education. Among other strong influences were printed books and the Protestant Reformation.

Outstanding artists emerged in several countries as the Renaissance spread north of the Italian Alps. Early advocates were the Flemish painter Jan van Eyck, whose works featured delicate realistic details, and Pieter Bruegel the Elder, famed for his large landscapes. Hieronymus Bosch, a Dutch painter, was known for his surrealistic religious paintings. The German Renaissance produced such renowned artists as Hans Holbein the

Younger, the Bavarian who travelled as far as England painting realistic portraits, and Albrecht Dürer, who painted figures in relaxed classical poses. In France, Jean Fouquet was the first artist to travel to Italy to experience the Renaissance. Jean Clouet the Elder and his son, Francois, who were miniaturist portrait painters, both became the chief painter to King Francis I.

JAN VAN EYCK (BEFORE 1395–1441)

Born in Maaseik (then named Eyck) near Maastricht into a wealthy and privileged family, Van Eyck's first known work was in 1422 in The Hague for the Count of Holland, John of Bavaria. He then became the court painter for Philip the Good, the Duke of Burgundy, at Bruges and Lille. In 1428, he travelled to Portugal to paint the duke's future wife, Isabella of Portugal and was given other diplomatic missions. He was praised for his religious subjects with disguised symbolism and

BELOW: Van Eyck's *The Adoration of the Mystic Lamb* was stolen by Napoleon then again several times during World War II.

for his portraits; *Portrait of a Man in a Red Turban* from 1433 is assumed to be a self-portrait.

Van Eyck used oil paints to highlight his interest in the effects of light on surfaces, which he painted in realistic and minute detail using a magnifying glass. His reputation grew throughout Europe for the method he developed of layering thin glazes of oil paint to create a striking realism. His masterpiece for the altar in the Ghent cathedral in 1432 was *The Adoration of the Mystic Lamb*, also known as 'The Ghent Altarpiece'. It was supposedly begun in the 1420s by his older brother Hubert, and on his death finished by Jan, but this is doubtful. The work is renowned for its rich colours and goldwork. It mixes the divine and human across 12 panels, with unusual scenes showing the angel visiting Mary in a room filled with details and Christ sitting enthroned in heaven instead of suffering on the cross.

Van Eyck's most recognized work is *The Arnolfini Portrait*, about the marriage of the merchant Giovanni Arnolfini and his wife. It has been in London's National Gallery since 1842. One of two figures shown in a mirror may be that of the artist. Van Eyck signed his paintings in a witty manner, and this one reads: 'Jan van Eyck was here 1434'. Several of his other signed works add his aristocratic motto: 'As best I can.'

BELOW: This, one of three self-portraits by Durer, was inscribed, 'I have thus painted myself. I was 26 years old. Albrecht Durer'.

ALBRECHT DÜRER (1471–1528)

Dürer was born in Nuremberg as one of 18 children and became an apprentice to his father, a goldsmith, and to a local painter, Michael Wolgemut, who produced woodcut illustrations for publications. Dürer's skills in creating details and subtlety of lines turned woodcuts and engravings into new art forms, beginning with his series of religious subjects including the woodcut *The Apocalypse* in 1498 and the engraving *Adam and Eve* in 1504, which depicts the

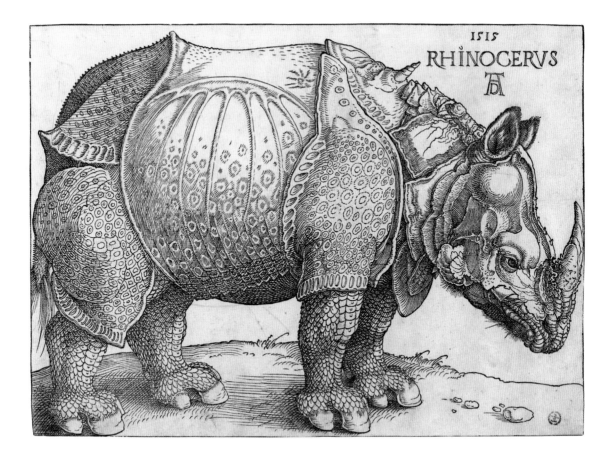

couple as perfectly formed humans in idealized poses. His painted works are mostly portraits, altarpieces and devotional images.

In 1512, he became the court painter to Maximilian I, the Holy Roman Emperor, who commissioned him to create a monumental woodcut that could be used to produce prints to enhance his image. Dürer's scenes of the emperor's military successes for *Triumphal Arch* were made on a surface measuring 10sqm (108sq ft), one of the largest woodcuts ever created. Between 1513 and 1514, he completed three engravings he called his *Meisterstiche* ('master prints'), each depicting an individual in a symbolic circumstance: *St Jerome in his Study*; *Melancholy* as a dejected winged creature; and *Knight, Death and the Devil* riding through a forest. In 1515, he made the fantastic woodcut *The Rhinoceros*, drawn from a German merchant's sketch.

His interest in the Renaissance and its humanism led to two trips to Italy (1494–95 and 1505–07) and another to the

ABOVE: Durer's *The Rhinoceros* was one of his most popular woodcuts with an estimated 4000 to 5000 prints sold in his lifetime.

'THE EYES AND EARS OF GERMANY'

ALBRECHT DÜRER'S HOME CITY of Nuremberg was the perfect centre for the northern Renaissance. Situated in the middle of Europe, it was home to numerous printing presses that rapidly spread the ideas of the Italian Renaissance.

Martin Luther called Nuremberg 'the eyes and ears of Germany'. It was also a hub for trade and manufacturing, making it a centre of wealth and culture that generated commissions and patronage from the city's great families for its many artists,

sculptors, printmakers and goldsmiths. Nuremberg promoted humanism through influential men like Willibald Pirckheimer (1470–1530), an affluent lawyer, writer and humanist whose home became a centre of learning. He was Dürer's closest friend, introducing the artist to other prominent humanists and loaning him money for his trip to Venice in 1505. Dürer featured Pirckheimer in many of his woodcuts, including *The Apocalypse*, and painted several portraits of him.

Netherlands (1520–21). During his first visit to Venice, he became intrigued with the works of Andrea Mantegna and Giovanni Bellini and with the idea of divine harmony and proportion. These experiences eventually led him to write a book on geometric theory in 1525 entitled *Instructions for Measuring with a Compass and Ruler*, becoming the first northern European artist to analyze perspective. He also wrote four books on human proportions, the first published in 1528.

Dürer was proud of his success and produced several self-portraits – sketched, painted and printed – that reveal the look of a self-confident artist. When he lay dying, a lock of hair was cut off and sent to one of his former pupils in Strasbourg; it now resides in the Vienna Academy of Art. Dürer's epitaph states: 'Whatever was mortal in Albrecht Dürer lies beneath this mound.'

PIETER BRUEGEL THE ELDER(1525–69)

Born in or near Breda, Bruegel settled as a young man in Antwerp, where he joined the Guild of St Luke and became a master painter in about 1551. After visiting Italy, he began a close relationship with the Antwerp publishing house At the Four Winds, where from 1555 to 1563 he made more than 40 designs for engravings in the manner of Hieronymus Bosch. He produced original and imaginative paintings, such as his popular *Netherlandish Proverbs* in 1559, showing people acting out more than 100 proverbs in the setting of a Flemish village, and *The Triumph of Death*, which depicts a skeleton army massacring helpless masses of people.

Bruegel's distinctive style used a large landscape depicting a narrative with people coming together in various groups, as in the crowded street of *Children's Games*, painted in 1560. This represented a departure from the approach of previous heroes of Renaissance art by focusing on the common lot of those living everyday lives, a humanistic approach that influenced later generations of artists. As a result, he was given the nickname 'Peasant Bruegel' for his many paintings of Flemish workers and

BELOW: In *Children's Games*, Bruegel depicted more than 250 children and about 84 games, some of which are still played today.

commoners. His flamboyant but well-designed depictions of peasants in their torn clothes show them, for example, celebrating in *The Dirty Bride or The Wedding of Mopsus and Nisu*, painted in 1570, and playing at a county fair in *The Kermis at Hoboken* in 1559. He also did a series of seasonal landscapes showing peasants at work, such as the winter scene of *Hunters in the Snow* in 1565, which captures the scope of life, with the men plodding along a hill overlooking cosy cottages and happy skaters.

Bruegel sired several other artists, none of whom matched his brilliance: his sons were Pieter Bruegel the Younger (c.1564 –1637), who copied his father's style and Jan Bruegel the Elder (1568–1625), who copied his lost works. Other lesser known artist descendants include Jan's son, Jan the Younger (1601–78).

IN SPAIN, EL GRECO WAS ADMIRED FOR HIS SENSITIVE PORTRAITS AND RECEIVED MANY RELIGIOUS COMMISSIONS.

EL GRECO (1541–1614)
He was born as Domenikos Theotokopoulos in Crete, then a Venetian possession, and studied art in Italy, but El Greco ('The Greek') settled in Toledo, Spain, in 1577 and spent the remainder of his life there, becoming a driving force in the Spanish Renaissance. In Venice, he trained under Titian and was influenced by Tintoretto. While there, he developed the colourful mannerist style, the sophisticated and highly finished art form that idealized the human body in twisting, muscular figures. By late 1570, he was in Rome studying the art of Michelangelo and Raphael. Either there or before he left Venice, he painted the masterpiece *Christ Healing the Blind*, showing Jesus anointing a man's eyes to restore his sight.

In Spain El Greco was admired for his sensitive portraits and received many religious commissions. King Philip II commissioned him to paint *The Martyrdom of Saint Maurice* (1580–82) but was displeased with the result, probably due to its shocking colours, and so ended their association. Then, from 1586 to 1588, El Greco produced another masterpiece, *The Burial of the Count of Orgaz*, showing St Augustine and St Stephen placing the count in his tomb. It demonstrates the artist's use of fluid brushstrokes,

surprising colours and the elongation of figures that suggests their spirituality. The figure of a young boy in the painting was El Greco's son, whose pocket handkerchief shows the artist's signature and the date of the boy's birth (1578).

El Greco's dramatic style and his appreciation of Byzantine art created a perfect fit for the Counter Reformation in Toledo. From 1590 he produced many more works for local churches and convents, including 25 featuring St Francis of Assisi (patron saint of Toledo), such as *Saint Francis and Brother Leo Meditating on Death*, painted about 1600. After his own death in 1614, his art became less popular and less of an influence on other painters, who found it difficult to follow his visionary subjects and idiosyncratic methods. 'I paint because the spirits whisper madly inside my head,' he once wrote. He was rescued from obscurity in the nineteenth century by critics and collectors, becoming an influence for later painters like Van Gogh, Cezanne and Picasso.

ABOVE: The upper left portion of El Greco's *Christ Healing the Blind* is unfinished. He painted two other versions of the subject.

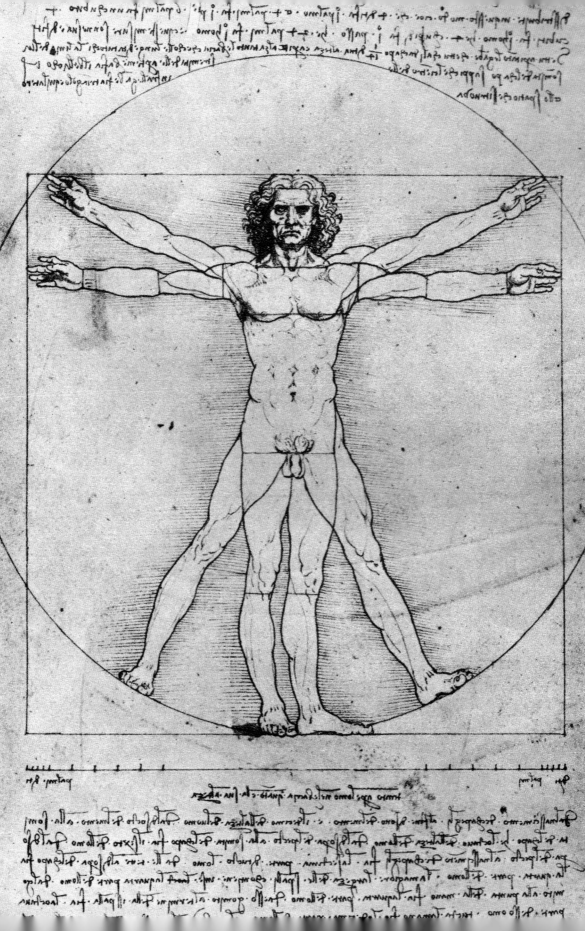

CHAPTER 3

Science and Medicine

While Renaissance artists and architects looked to the classical world for inspiration, scientists and doctors were more interested in new techniques. They did review ancient texts in their fields, but for them, the value of the Renaissance was its encouragement of humanistic enquiry and practical experiments that improved lives.

ONE PARTICULAR invention – Johannes Gutenberg's printing press, with its movable type – was responsible for the rapid spread of knowledge in all fields during the Renaissance. Without the circulation of printed papers and books, other inventions would have gone virtually unnoticed. Some of these printed materials were classic texts on science and medicine that had been discovered, translated, discussed and printed for wide distribution; with Italy producing the most books by 1500, despite often relying on German printing presses. Early Greek and Roman studies were reprinted with revisions and additions in such fields as anatomy, geography, zoology, botany, astronomy and mathematics. New ideas began to replace ancient medical practices, like the rejection in the early sixteenth century of the theory that a body had four 'humours' that caused diseases if they became unbalanced, and

OPPOSITE: Leonardo's *Vitruvian Man* was proportionally correct. He applied ideas of proportion by the Roman architect Vitruvius to the human form.

the 'miasma' theory that said diseases were caused by vapours from the earth or air.

Printed texts also promoted much erroneous information; for example, popularizing the ancient pseudoscience of astrology, so that horoscopes were cast to plan important events like weddings. Doctors also consulted the stars and planets before prescribing medicines or performing bloodlettings. Old religious beliefs sometimes became entangled in Renaissance science, as when mathematics was used to explain the unity of God and his universe.

Renaissance minds were active and innovative, leading to inventions that remain part of modern life. Among these are the telescope, compound microscope, submarine, marine compass, mechanical clock, portable clock, eyeglasses, wallpaper, flushing toilet, screwdriver, cannons firing metal balls using gunpowder and double-entry bookkeeping; while new practices included the adoption of Arabic numerals. Leonardo da Vinci also contributed

sketches and designs of inventions that were
not actually produced during the Renaissance,
including the helicopter, parachute, armoured car,
revolving bridge and machine gun.

ASTRONOMY

Major advances were made by Renaissance
astronomers, several of whom were outside Italy.
Nicolaus Copernicus was a Polish astronomer
who made the astounding claim that the Earth
and other planets orbit the sun, not the other way
around. This defied 'facts' in the Bible and existing
astronomical texts. He also deduced that the Earth
rotates on its axis to create day and night and
that its axis slowly changes direction to cause the
precession of the equinoxes (their movement along the plane of
the Earth's orbit). These theories were included in his essay *Little
Commentary*, written sometime between 1508 and 1514. He
expanded his theories in *Six Books Concerning the Revolutions
of the Heavenly Orbs*, published in 1543, the year of his death.

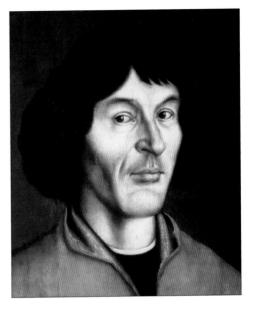

ABOVE: Copernicus' fame
as an astronomer even
prompted the Pope to
seek his advice to help the
Catholic Church improve
its calendar.

Copernicus' idea of a
heliocentric universe (with the
sun at its centre) was publicly
ridiculed and disbelieved,
but two astronomers who
modified it with enthusiasm
were the Dane Tycho Brahe
(1546–1601) and German
Johannes Kepler (1571–1630).

Making careful
observations of stars before
the invention of the telescope,
Brahe's most famous discovery
was that of a new star in
the Cassiopeia constellation
and moving comets that
proved the heavens were

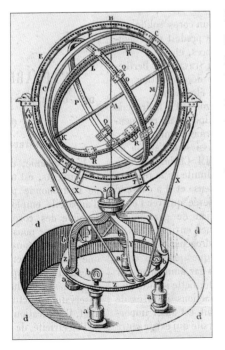

LEFT: The astrolabe was
one of Brahe's oldest
astronomical instruments.
It had existed since the
second century BC to
measure the sun's position.

not fixed and perfect. Using only a compass and sextant, he created the most accurate star charts then seen, based on precise observations of more than 1000 stars he and his assistants, apprentices and family made at his observatory on the Danish island of Hven (which is today part of Sweden). Brahe, who admired the mathematics behind Copernicus' heliocentric theory, still believed in an immovable Earth orbited by the sun and moon but thought the other five known planets of his time revolved around the sun and all orbited the Earth. He presented this theory in 1588 in a treatise called *De Mundi Aetherei Recentioribus Phaenomenis* (*On the Most Recent Phenomena of the Etherial World*).

BELOW: **A statue of Galileo Galilei outside Florence's Uffizi Gallery was sculpted in 1851 by the Florentine sculptor Aristodemo Costoli.**

Kepler was an assistant of Brahe's and used his observations to prove the orbit of Mars was an ellipse. This had been a question Brahe had asked him to answer, but Brahe withheld most of his own collected observations in case Kepler used them to prove Copernicus' heliocentric idea. However, when Brahe died his work passed down to Kepler.

Using those calculations, Kepler devised three laws for the orbits of planets that supported Copernicus: first, planets move in an ellipse around the sun; second, a planet moves faster when closest to the sun and more slowly when farthest from it; and third, a precise mathematical relationship exists between a planet's distance from the sun and the time it takes to complete a revolution around it.

THE TELESCOPE

One supporter of Copernicus with special influence was Galileo Galilei (1564–1642), the Italian astronomer and mathematician who used the newly invented telescope to verify the Earth circling the sun, even though he believed planets moved in circular orbits.

A telescope had been produced in the Netherlands in 1608 and Galileo became aware of the 'Danish perspective

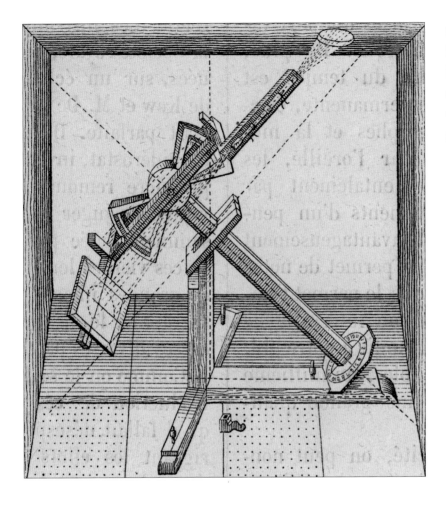

LEFT: Galileo's telescope had a convex objective lens and a concave eyepiece. The Milky Way was among objects he focused upon.

glass'. He built his own in 1609 and refined it, increasing the magnification from three times larger to 30 times. With this, he was able to see that the moon was not a perfect sphere but had various features, Jupiter had moons, and the sun had 'imperfections' (sunspots) whose movements demonstrated that it rotated. These discoveries convinced him of the sun-centred solar system. He sketched his observations and quickly published his findings in 1610 in a treatise, *Sidereus Nuncius* (*Starry Messenger*), which was rapidly distributed throughout Europe.

In 1614, Galileo was accused of heresy for this, and two years later the Catholic Church forbade him from teaching or promoting the heliocentric theory. Nevertheless, he published his book *Dialogue Concerning the Two Chief World Systems*, which set out the pros and cons for Copernicus' ideas, and in 1632 he

ABOVE: Galileo's inquisition trial in Rome in 1633 is depicted in this painting in 1857 by the Italian artist Chistiano Banti.

was again condemned for heresy and ordered to appear before the Inquisition in Rome. There, he was convicted and sentenced to life imprisonment. Instead, he was forced to publicly recant his belief in the heliocentric theory and given a reduced but permanent sentence of house arrest in his villa near Florence. In 1638, four years before he died, Galileo's book was published again.

In 1992, Pope John Paul II announced that Galileo had been correct, an admission given more than 350 years after his condemnation by the Catholic Inquisition.

LEONARDO'S WAR MACHINES

Leonardo da Vinci detested war, calling it 'a bestial madness', but he lived among the warring city states, and his patrons insisted on him creating new and powerful machines for both defence and attack.

Perhaps his most awesome design was for a giant crossbow, called the *ballista*, which would intimidate the enemy. The huge bows of thin interlocking wood rested on six wheels and were drawn back by winding gears he also invented. The machine was triggered by a release catch activated either by striking the firing pin with a mallet or by pulling a rope. It was able to fire anything that would cause danger, from rocks to the cluster bombs he had invented.

THE CATAPULT COULD ALSO THROW LEAD BALLS, FLAMING OBJECTS AND EVEN DEAD BODIES RIDDEN WITH DISEASES.

Another device for attacking castles was Leonardo's improved version of the existing catapult, which was slow and cumbersome. His version rapidly fired ammunition that rested at the end of a long swinging arm, and he designed a projectile with two tail fins that could carry gunpowder to explode on contact. The catapult could also throw lead balls, flaming objects and even dead bodies ridden with diseases. It was tensely tightened by a rope wound about a drum that was turned and then triggered by striking the firing pin with a mallet.

One invention for closer fighting was Leonardo's armoured tank, which could strike fear by driving straight into the enemy.

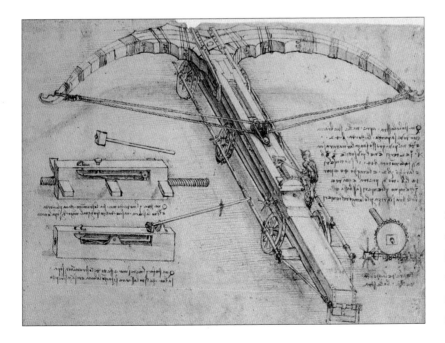

LEFT: Leonardo's giant crossbow was one of his inventions to intimidate the enemy, and his drawing added even more psychological fear.

It was operated by eight soldiers using hand cranks to move in several directions. Others inside the tank fired light cannon arranged on a wheeled platform that could turn 360 degrees. Over this was a metal cover slanted to a point to deflect enemy fire and with a viewing turret on top. The tank had a major flaw, namely, the hand cranks went in opposite directions, making forward motion impossible. Some have suggested this was intentional, since Leonardo was an accomplished engineer and, being a pacifist, hoped his tank would never be used.

Leonardo called his projected machine gun an 'organ' because its 33 barrels resembled the pipes of an organ. The weapon had three rows of 11 barrels, all attached together and fixed to a frame with wheels so it would rotate. The first row of loaded small-calibre guns was fired, and the frame then rotated to bring up the next 11 from beneath to be fired. Soldiers operating the device could fire a row while letting the previous one cool and loading the waiting one. This continuous action would overcome the slow loading and firing of traditional cannon. Leonardo's guns were breech-loaded and water-cooled, features ahead of their time.

Leonardo's idea for a cluster bomb resembled the concept for a modern weapon. He envisaged an exploding cannonball that would shatter into small deadly pieces and set off other cannonballs, all contained in an outer shell. He explained the process, writing that 'when the cannonball falls, the nucleus sets fire to the other balls, and the central ball explodes and shatters the others that catch fire in the time it takes to say a "Hail Mary"'.

BELOW: These technical sketches of a prototype machine gun show Leonardo's attention to detail, providing ample information without written instructions.

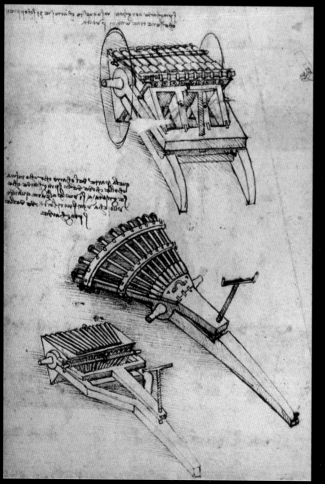

THE ANIMAL LOVER

DESPITE THE AGGRESSIVE IMAGE, Leonardo had gained for his in-demand military machines, the artist was a pacifist and defended animal rights. Walking through a market, he would purchase a bird in a cage and release it. He often stated that humans are not 'king of the animals', an opinion that contradicted the biblical account in Genesis. Leonardo deplored that we only raise animals for slaughter and he refused to eat meat from an early age. He wrote that 'the time will come when men such as I will look upon the murder of animals as they now look upon the murder of men'. He equally criticized using animals for work, saying that donkeys are 'repaid by hunger and thirst, pain and blows, goads and curses and loud abuse'. He also practised what he preached, using men instead of horses to power his armoured tank because the machine would frighten the animals.

For naval warfare, Leonardo invented the double-hulled ship and underwater diving gear. The addition of a second hull would keep a ship afloat if its outer hull were holed, as when rammed during an attack or penetrated by wreckage.

The diving gear would allow someone to attack a vessel from beneath the surface. The breathing apparatus consisted of cane tubes that were joined by leather joints, while rings of steel protected them from water pressure. The tubes were attached to the face mask and the other end to a float keeping its opening above water. A leather bag was used to urinate. Another design showed air stored in a leather wineskin kept in a pouch of a coat. The diver also took along sandbags for ballast, a knife, a rope and a horn to signal that his dive was completed.

UP IN THE AIR

Leonardo's most unattainable ideas were his designs for airborne travel by flying machine, helicopter and parachute. He was inspired by watching kites and by the flying animal world, naming birds and bats as examples. He produced some 500 sketches of flying machines and bird flights.

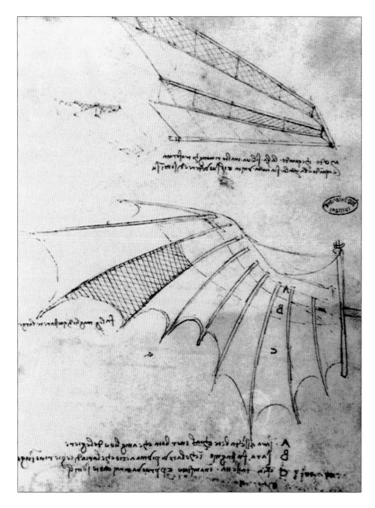

ABOVE: Leonardo's design for a human-powered flying machine was sketched about 1485. It followed his observations of birds and bats.

His flying machine also called the ornithopter (an aircraft that flies by flapping its wings), had wings spanning 10m (33ft) that were made of silk in pine frames and pointed like a bat's. The pilot would lie prone on a board in the centre and pedal a crank that moved rods and pulleys to flap the wings. A hand crank was available for additional power. In another version of an ornithopter, he had the pilot standing. Considering a human's weight and that the machine was without an engine, Leonardo's invention would never be able to take off from the ground. His helicopter had a rotor blade 2m (6ft) in diameter and a supporting section held together by reeds. To achieve lift -off, four men were to stand in a circular platform in the centre, and each hold a vertical wooden shaft connected to a central one reaching up to the 'blades'. Pushing the four shafts would rotate the blades to screw the helicopter upwards.

Anticipating the friction this would cause between the blade apparatus and the platform, Leonardo invented the first modern ball bearings. Even so, the weight of the helicopter, like his flying machine, meant it would never be able to overcome the force of gravity and leave the ground.

Leonardo's idea for a parachute consisted of a sealed linen cloth about 7m (23ft) in width and the same in depth. It was opened by wooden poles about 7m (23ft) in length and arranged in a triangle. He noted that a person using the parachute could jump from any height and land without injury. He never tested it, but in 2000 Adrian Nichols, a skydiver, built a prototype of the design and tested it, reporting that it worked perfectly and even provided a smoother descent than a modern parachute.

SUBMARINES

Around 1515 Leonardo sketched a design for a submarine but kept it a secret, worrying about 'the evil nature of men who practise assassination at the bottom of the sea'. The first true design for a submarine was drawn up by the British mathematician William Bourne in 1578. It used waterproof leather to totally cover the wooden frame. Hand vices reduced the vessel's size to submerge, and oars provided the forward motion.

The Dutch inventor Cornelis Drebbel built the first workable submarine that he called a 'diving boat' and conducted trials from 1620 to 1624 in London's Thames River. He tested his third model successfully for three hours at a depth of 5m (15ft) from Westminster to Greenwich. This was in front of King James I, who briefly visited onboard, and thousands of spectators. The entire vessel was sealed with greased leather and in the middle was a waterproof hatch. It could carry 16 people who sat on pigskin bladders used for ballast, with pipes leading outside and a rope to tie off each empty bladder. The rope was untied for

BELOW: This drawing imagines how Cornelius Drebbel's wooden diving boat looked. His own sketches and written plans have not survived.

intake of water to fill the bladder and submerge the submarine, and the passengers had to squeeze the water out of the bladders to resurface. Six oars were used to provide the forward motion underwater. Air inside came from two tubes using floats to lift their upper ends to the surface.

CORNELIS DREBBEL (1572–1633)

Drebbel was born in Alkmaar, a town in the Netherlands, and was first apprenticed to a famous engraver, Hendrick Goltzius, who also encouraged his interest in alchemy. Drebbel became an accomplished engraver. He married in 1595 and had four surviving children. In 1604 the family moved to England at the invitation of King James I, who attached Drebbel to the court of Henry, Prince of Wales. Drebbel amazed the royalty with his invention of a perpetual motion clock mounted in a globe. It told the time, date and season, reacting to atmospheric pressure and temperature.

As his fame grew, he was invited to Prague in 1610 by Rudolf II, the Holy Roman Emperor, but Drebbel was arrested the next year when Rudolf was overthrown, and it took the intervention of the English court to secure his freedom. At about this time Drebbel began building three submarines, each one larger than the last and won renown after the impressive trial of his 'diving boat' in 1620. He is also credited with inventing an improved thermometer, a scarlet dye, the construction of a compound microscope (having become an expert lens grinder), and the use of a thermostat to control the temperature of a self-regulating oven.

When James I died in 1625 the new king, Charles I, appointed Drebbel to the Office of Ordnance to invent secret weapons for the navy, one of which

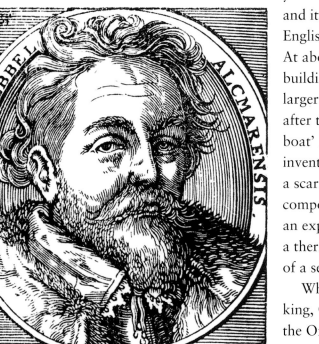

BELOW: Contemporaries described Cornelius Drebbel as looking like a handsome Dutch farmer, having a sharp wit and gentle manners.

MARKING TIME

DURING THE EARLY RENAISSANCE large mechanical clocks would ring the hours, but anyone that lived out of earshot of tower bells had to rely on a sundial (of which pocket versions existed), or estimate the sun's position, to judge the approximate time. This was changed by the famous architect Filippo Brunelleschi, who was also an excellent clockmaker. He introduced a portable mechanical clock in 1410 in Florence, having designed the coil spring that made it possible. This led to the table clock and then the first true watches began to appear about 1500 and were worn by rich owners mainly to display their wealth.

LEFT: This portable silver and gold watch was owned by someone of great affluence in the sixteenth or seventeenth century.

was an unsuccessful floating bomb. By 1629 Drebbel had lapsed into poverty, and he survived by running an alehouse under London Bridge.

THE FLUSH TOILET

Before the Renaissance latrines, which carried waste away on a non-stop stream of water, had already existed for 5000 years or more. The inside chamber pot also existed, and its contents were often dumped on the street from an upper window.

The first flush toilet was invented by the English courtier Sir John Harington (1561–1612), the godson of Elizabeth I. In 1592 he built one for the queen at Richmond Palace and one for himself at his house near Bath, where he had been exiled from court for telling lewd stories. His 'water closet' consisted of an oval bowl 60cm (2ft) deep that was covered with pitch, resin and wax as waterproofing, underneath a raised cistern and pipe that carried water down to flush the waste when a valve was opened.

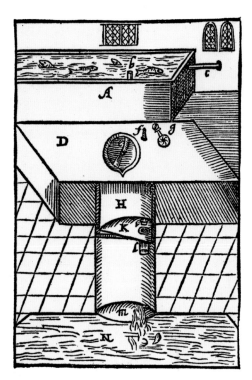

One flush required 28 litres (7.5 gallons) of water, but Sir John claimed that up to 20 people could use the toilet between flushes.

Despite his efforts, the public ignored his new convenience, perhaps because of its foul odours. This problem was not solved until 1775 when the S-shaped pipe under the bowl was invented by the Scottish watchmaker Alexander Cummings (1733–1814), who became the first person to patent a design for a flush toilet.

MATHEMATICS

The importance of numbers was concisely summed up by the Renaissance philosopher Giovanni Pico della Mirandola, who wrote: 'By number a way is had to be searching out and understanding of everything to be known.'

Among the ancient Greek writings recovered during the Renaissance were mathematical texts, preserved as Byzantine documents in Arabic translations. These included the valuable works of Euclid, known as 'the father of geometry', whose *Elements* is the longest surviving mathematical work, and Archimedes, who wrote explanations of arithmetic, geometry and mechanics. Some of this knowledge is taught today without revision, such as Euclid's Pythagorean theorem that the square of the hypotenuse of a right-angled triangle is equal to the sum of the squares of the two sides.

An important Renaissance innovation that began in the thirteenth century was the adaptation of Arabic numerals to replace Roman ones, thus adding the zero and fractions written as decimals. There had been some resistance to using the Arabic system, which was invented in Hindu India but received its name from the translated Arabic texts of mathematics and astronomy. In 1280 the city of Florence banned its use by bankers, believing the zero would cause mistakes in calculations and might even be used as a secret code. Nevertheless, the system was too simple to be rejected and quickly spread through Europe, where the calculations with Roman numerals were made with an abacus. Around 1495, Leonardo de Vinci wrote in his notebook: 'Learn multiplication from the root from Maestro Luca.' He was referring to Luca Pacioli, a Franciscan friar and mathematician who became a famous accountant and the father of double-entry bookkeeping, although this had existed much earlier. In 1494 Pacioli set down the precise details of mathematics in *Summary of Arithmetic, Geometry, Proportions and Proportionality*, an enormous book of 615 pages that included a clear description of double-entry bookkeeping. It was translated throughout Europe and had a great influence. In 1509, he added the book *Divine Proportion*, which was illustrated by Leonardo.

LEFT: A woodcut from a 1503 book shows how faster calculations were made by Hindu-Arabic numerals compared to an abacus.

LUCA PACIOLI (1445–1517)

Born in Tuscany in the town of Sansepolcro, Pacioli became a tutor to a merchant's three sons in Venice and in 1470 wrote an arithmetic book dedicated to them. By the early 1470s, he had moved to Rome and became a friar in the Franciscan order. Between 1477 and 1480 he taught mathematics at the University of Perugia and wrote a large unpublished textbook on the subject. He later taught at the universities of Naples and Rome, before returning to Sansepolcro in 1489.

HE WAS ABLE TO WRITE A MAJOR BOOK ON ALGEBRA, AS WELL AS GIVE THE FIRST CLINICAL DESCRIPTION OF TYPHUS FEVER.

He published his definitive book, *Summary of Arithmetic, Geometry, Proportions and Proportionality*, in 1494 in Venice. It contained his description of double-entry bookkeeping and the first Italian language explanation of algebra. It also described the rigorous attention required for an accurate accountancy system. Pacioli explained how to keep an inventory, which had been neglected by many businessmen, and the necessity of keeping a daily record of transactions. For the

RIGHT: Luca Pacioli is shown demonstrating a theorem by Euclid in this 1495 portrait by the Italian painter Jacopo de Barbari.

RENAISSANCE MAGIC

LUCA PACIOLI WAS ALSO an amateur magician, and wrote a book on magic and mathematics that gave instructions on writing in code and how to perform card tricks, juggling and fire-eating, along with mathematical puzzles. This oldest magic text, *De Viribus Quantitatis* (*On the Powers of Numbers*), was written between 1496 and 1508 and hidden away in the University of Bologna until it was finally translated into English in 2008.

Pacioli's card trick involved placing a boy in another room and having him guess which cards were touched by people, with the answers secretly placed on the cards. Much more dangerous than the card trick was washing one's hands in molten lead, with the feat involving first soaking the hands in cool well water containing 'ground rock alum'.

The book includes mathematical problems and puzzles involving numbers, much like ones printed in modern newspapers. The participation of Leonardo da Vinci is evident, with some of the puzzles found in his notebooks, and by Pacioli's comment: 'Well Leonardo, you can do more of this on your own'.

latter, he recommended a journal, a memorandum notebook and a ledger for the double entries.

In 1497 Pacioli moved to Milan at the invitation of Duke Ludovico Sforza. There he met Leonardo da Vinci, who was the duke's court painter and engineer. They became close friends and lived together, with Pacioli teaching Leonardo mathematics and Leonardo instructing him in art. They were driven from the city two years later when it was taken by the French. The two men kept in touch for a while, until Pacioli returned to Sansepolcro in 1510. He lived there for the remainder of his life, with one visit to Rome to lecture in 1514.

GIROLAMO CARDANO (1501–76)

An illegitimate son of a Milan lawyer, Cardano became the most brilliant mathematician of his time; Leonardo da Vinci consulted him on geometry. Also a renowned physician, he was a true Renaissance man and therefore able to write a major book on algebra as well as give the first clinical description of typhus fever. His father left him a small bequest which he quickly spent, forcing him to turn to gambling – an obsession throughout his life. He received a medical degree in 1526 and moved in 1534 to Milan, where he was turned down several times for membership to the College of Physicians. Living in poverty, he returned to gambling until finding employment as a mathematics teacher. He also treated patients with such skills that he was finally admitted to the College of Physicians in 1539, becoming rector there and winning fame for his medical knowledge, which attracted European heads of state and wealthy patients.

In 1539, he also published two mathematics books and became a leader in that field, doing the first calculations with complex numbers. In 1543 he was appointed Professor of Medicine at Pavia University, and in 1545 he published his excellent mathematical book, *Ars Magna* (*The Great Art*), which included important solutions by others of the cubic and quartic equations solved by others. His influential books included *The Book on Games of Chance*, which presented the first systematic calculations of probabilities, and *The Subtlety of Things* about inventions and physical experiments. He also wrote about astronomy, philosophy, geology and theology, and published two encyclopedias of natural science dealing with diverse topics such as cosmology, mechanics and cryptology.

Then, at the height of his success, he suffered what he termed his 'crowning misfortune', when his favourite son was executed in 1560 for poisoning his wife. Two years later, Cardano became a professor in

RIGHT: Girolmo Cardano also made an important improvement to the camera obscura by adding a bi-convex lens that sharpened the image.

Bologna and in 1570 was imprisoned for heresy for casting the horoscope of Christ. Released within a few months, after he privately abjured, he was forbidden from holding a university position and from publishing his work. His last book was his autobiography, *The Book of My Life*.

GEOGRAPHY

Interest in distant seas and lands increased dramatically in the Renaissance, as Italians became more involved in trade and exploration. Since few maps existed and those that did were unreliable, discussions about geography were rife with rumours and speculation. This began to change after two classic Greek manuscripts were brought to Florence. One was by the second-century Roman geographer Ptolemy (Claudius Ptolemaeus), who had been born in Greece and lived in Alexandria. His work *Geography* was brought from Constantinople in 1400 and translated into Latin in 1410, revealing his knowledge of the subject in 150 AD. Another find was *Geographica*, 17 volumes written in 7 BC by the Greek Strabo, who studied geography in Rome and travelled extensively, as far as Syria and Ethiopia.

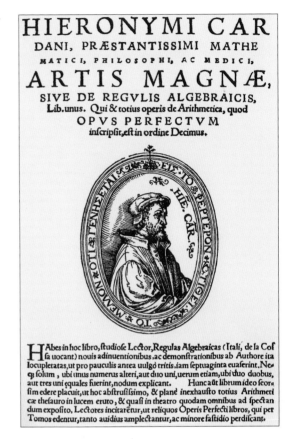

ABOVE: Cardano's *Ars Magna* emphasized the rules of algebra, part of the original title. A second edition was published in 1570.

These seminal texts inspired Florentine scholars such as Poggio Bracciolini and the Florentine cosmographer Paolo dal Pozzo Toscanelli (1397–1482). The latter believed the world was round and one could sail west to reach India. These ideas were taken up by Christopher Columbus, who was sent a letter that Toscanelli had written to the king of Portugal about the western route.

By the fifteenth century, the invention of printing boosted the distribution of maps, which had become crucial in the age of exploration. These included navigational charts pointing out shoreline features and dangers for sailors. In 1492, the year

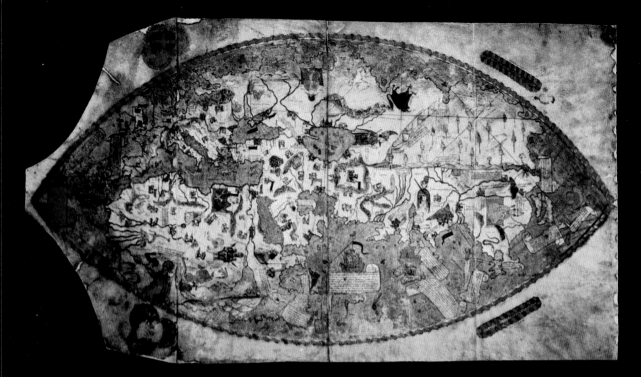

ABOVE: This world map by Paolo Toscanelli in 1457, which underestimated the Earth's circumference, was carried by Columbus on his voyage.

of Columbus' voyage, the German geographer and navigator Martin Behaim (1459–1507) completed a globe, but much of it was inaccurate. The first world map, *Universalis Cosmographia*, was produced in 1507 by the German cartographers Martin Waldseemüller (1470–1520) and Matthias Ringmann (1482–1511). It was the first to name the New World as 'America' to honour the Italian explorer Amerigo Vespucci.

A new standard for map-making was set in 1544 by the German cartographer Sebastian Münster (1488–1552), whose *Geographia* was the earliest true German depiction of the world. In 1569 a cylindrical projection map of the world was published by Gerardus Mercator (1512–94), a Flemish geographer. This type of map, which projects the world as a sphere on to a flat surface, is still produced and bears his name.

POGGIO BRACCIOLINI (1380–1459)

Born Gian Francesco Poggio Bracciolini in Tuscany, this humanist scholar and writer worked in Florence copying manuscripts, during which time he invented a round, formal 'humanist' script that eventually became the prototype of Roman fonts. He moved to Rome in 1403, becoming secretary to Pope Boniface IX, the first of four popes he served in this way. He then began searching in monasteries as far as France, Switzerland and Germany for classical writings, finding many Latin texts, including several of Cicero's orations and the last surviving manuscript of *De Rerum Natura* (*On the Nature of Things*) by the Roman poet and philosopher Lucretius.

In 1418, he went to England for five years to locate more manuscripts and returned to Rome as papal secretary to continue the search. Among his own influential writings was *Invectivae* (*Invectives*), which he used to make witty and scandalous attacks on the clergy and literary rivals in their ongoing quarrels.

Poggio Bracciolini also collected ancient sculptures for the garden of his villa in Florence. In 1453 he became Chancellor of Florence and spent his remaining years writing a history of that city.

MORE ACCURATE KNOWLEDGE OF ANATOMY AND DISEASE WAS BECOMING AVAILABLE, LEADING TO THE QUESTIONING OF GALEN.

BELOW: Poggio Bracciolini's prototype for Roman fonts came as he copied classic manuscripts in his beautiful handwriting.

MEDICINE

The impetus behind the Renaissance came from scholars who were discovering the classic texts of ancient Greece and Rome; medicine, however, was a field that had never been 'lost' due to the reputation of Galen (130 AD–210 AD), the Greek physician and surgeon who lived in Rome. His medical writings, translated in the Middle Ages, had been in constant use and Renaissance scholars did new translations, resulting in the publication of almost 600 editions of his books. Although physicians continued to follow his conclusions and advice, more accurate knowledge of anatomy and disease was becoming available, leading to the questioning of Galen's authority,

such as his belief in bloodletting and that a person's health depended on four humours. Disputing his methods, however, was controversial and resisted by most physicians.

The major source of new medical knowledge was the increase in the dissection of bodies. This practice was previously condemned by the Catholic Church, but its restrictions were

SEA MONSTERS

RENAISSANCE CARTOGRAPHERS OFTEN DECORATED their maps with fantastic monsters looking in from the margins or endangering sailors in unexplored areas. Among those that made frequent appearances were sea dragons, great serpents, monstrous whales and mermaids. Mapmakers drew these from their own imaginations, from the fantastic tales told by sailors, or by copying creatures in books or on medieval maps. People accepted that these imaginary monsters were added for decorative amusement, but their images were a powerful reminder to explorers of the unknown terrors that could be waiting.

Depicted is one of the sea monsters thought to dwell in the 'Sea of Darkness' south and west of Europe.

eased during the Renaissance, allowing a greater understanding of anatomy. Dissections were even carried out by the artists Leonardo and Michelangelo. Another source of advanced information about diseases and their treatments came from Islamic texts brought to Italy and the west by Muslim scholars after the fall of Constantinople in 1453.

Among those physicians who replaced old existing theories were Switzerland's Paracelsus (1493–1541), who founded toxicology; Italy's Girolamo Fracastoro (1478–1553), who said pathogens caused disease; England's William Harvey (1578–1657), who described how the heart circulated blood; and France's Ambroise Paré (1510–90), who founded modern forensic pathology and invented surgical instruments.

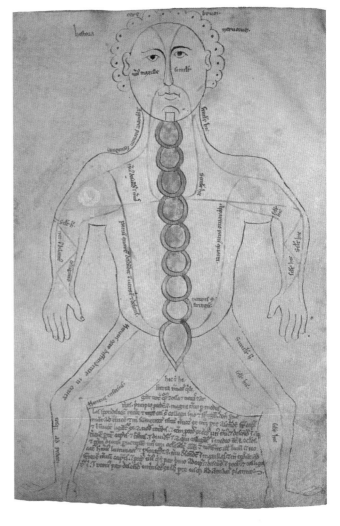

ABOVE: This second-century anatomy chart by Galen was basic, untested and incorrect due to a taboo on human dissections.

PARACELSUS (1493–1541)

Advances in Renaissance medicine sometimes included the powers of primitive folk beliefs. One advocate of both medical advances and folk medicine was the Swiss physician and alchemist Paracelsus, whose real name was Theophrastus Aureolus Bombastus von Hohenheim. Born near Zurich as the son of a physician, he studied medicine in Italy, receiving his doctorate in 1516 from the University of Ferrara. He became a surgeon with the Venetian army, travelling around Europe and as far as the British Isles, Russia and Egypt. Along the way he became influenced by folk medicines, saying: 'I have not been ashamed to learn from tramps, butchers and barbers.' He became well known for doubting the theory of four humours controlling the body's health, urging physicians to rely instead

FAMOSO·DOCTOR   PARESELSVS.

ABOVE: **This portrait of Paracelsus was by the Flemish artist Quentin Metysus, his contemporary. It is a copy of the lost original.**

on medical experiments with chemicals. He introduced metals and minerals as cures, such as using metal mercury to cure syphilis.

He founded the field of toxicology, targeting a specific location of a disease for measured doses of chemicals, and emphasized the importance of harmony between man and nature, changing some prescriptions according to the planets' alignments. Paracelsus called God 'the great magician' but also believed in fairies and gnomes. In 1526 he became Professor of Medicine at the University of Basel in Switzerland. He gave lectures dressed in an alchemist's leather apron and burned the books of famous ancient physicians, including Galen. For his unconventional beliefs, he was exiled from Basel in 1538 and died three years later in Austria.

GIROLAMO FRACASTORO (1478–1553)

Fracastoro was born in Verona and became a Renaissance man who knew astronomy, geology, geography, philosophy, mathematics and anatomy. He received a medical degree from the University of Padua in 1502 and that year became an instructor in logic and soon afterwards in medicine, becoming friends with the astronomer Copernicus, who was studying medicine there.

Fracastoro established a practice in Verona in 1509 and, from 1525 to 1530, he published a three-part poem giving 'the French disease' the name 'syphilis' and saying it could be cured with mercury. This made his name throughout Europe, where it was translated more than 100 times.

A BLOODY CURE

BLOODLETTING, THE CURE COMMONLY practised by surgeons for nearly 2000 years, persisted during the Renaissance. Galen had believed blood was the dominant humour, so he advocated the procedure and specified the illnesses it would cure, such as headaches, fevers and apoplexy. He considered the cause of these to be too much blood, so surgeons would cut the patient's vein and drain out some blood ('breathing a vein'). Different parts of the body were bled depending on the disease, and Galen even linked different veins to parts of the body. If overdone, bloodletting could cause anaemia or even death.

Renaissance surgeons stubbornly held onto these views, believing both Galen and Hippocrates had practised bloodletting. Jacobus Sylvius (1478–1555), the French physician and anatomist, said of the two that 'they had never written anything in physiology or other parts of medicine that was not entirely true'. Sylvius even gave names to blood vessels that are still used today, such as jugular, axillary and femoral. The only major controversy among Renaissance surgeons was whether bloodletting should be carried out on the same side as the disease or on the opposite one.

BELOW: The horror and fear of bloodletting was often depicted in Renaissance art but this failed to eliminate the ancient practice.

Aderlaßtafel ca. 1480. Holzschnitt. München, Kupferstichkabinet.

He became the personal physician to Pope Paul III, who made him medical adviser to the three sessions of the Council of Trent from 1545 to 1563. Fracastoro convinced the council to leave Trent because of the risk from the plague and also to reassemble in Bologna.

In 1547 Fracastoro published his idea of contagious diseases in *De Contagione et Contagiosis Morbis* (*On Contagion and Contagious Diseases*), naming minute germs as the cause. He also said they could be transferred to others by direct and indirect contacts, even through the air at long distances. This was nearly 300 years before Louis Pasteur, the French microbiologist, identified bacteria.

THE MOST POPULAR 'REMEDIES' WERE BLOODLETTING TO REMOVE AN EXCESS OF BLOOD AND LAXATIVES TO PURGE THE BODY.

THE FOUR HUMOURS

The ancient Greek philosophers and physicians Aristotle, Hippocrates and Galen promoted the idea of four humours controlling the body, an idea that came under attack during the Renaissance. It had been based on the belief that human and animal behaviour was determined by the four elements of earth, water, air and fire, along with the conditions of cold, heat, moistness and dryness. The third influence came from the humours, which were of prime interest to physicians. The four humours and the characteristics they created were: black bile from the spleen, causing a person to be melancholic; yellow bile from the gall bladder, causing a choleric nature; phlegm from the brain, leading to a phlegmatic nature; and blood from the heart for a sanguine nature.

The humours were a major influence on medical practices for centuries, and based on the belief that their balance was essential for good health, while an imbalance would cause disease. Treatments were designed to restore this balance, and these were unpleasant. The most popular 'remedies' were bloodletting to remove an excess of blood and laxatives to purge the body. Following Galen's advice in his three books *On the Power of Foods*, which matched foods to humours, doctors prescribed particular foods to correct a humoral imbalance. Thus, fever

OPPOSITE: Images of the four humours appeared in 1486 in the *Four Humours Guide Book of the Barber Surgeons of York.*

would be treated with cold foods like a salad. Shakespeare reflected this idea in *The Taming of the Shrew* by showing Petruchio snatching roasted meat away from Katherine because 'ourselves are choleric'.

Physicians continued to treat the humours throughout the Renaissance, but disbelief occurred among some of the practitioners. The Flemish surgeon and anatomist Andreas Vesalius (1514–64) pointed out mistakes Galen had made, while the Swiss physician Paracelsus introduced chemicals to treat illness and provoked outrage by burning Galen's books, saying he had made several errors.

ANATOMY AND DISSECTIONS BY ARTISTS

Renaissance painters and sculptors seldom had opportunities to view nude humans and fewer yet to dissect them to gain knowledge of how a body was put together. Some relied on nude or semi-nude models to understand how muscles and tendons lay beneath the skin. The Florentine Academy of Art had a course on anatomy that students were required to attend. This normally involved attending public dissections by physicians and sketching the results. Some physicians made agreements with artists, allowing them to participate in dissections in return for using their anatomical sketches in their books on the subject.

A PROBLEM WITH NEW FOODS

IT WAS SIMPLE FOR Renaissance physicians to match foods to correct the four humours. The second-century Greek physician Galen had described and classified them, but the arrival of new products from around the world that had been unknown to him created dissent. Cocoa, tea and coffee had arrived by the sixteenth century, causing arguments over how they could be used in medical treatments. Some physicians prescribed coffee for its heating effect, while others used it to cool the body because it dried up fluids. Cocoa posed a problem when sugar was added for drinking chocolate. Without sugar, it was classified as a bitter, dry food that could treat phlegmatic problems, but doctors argued over whether the sweet version, considered 'moist', could be used in the same way.

One of the first artists to dissect cadavers was the Florentine painter, engraver and sculptor Antonio del Pollaiuolo (*c*.1432–98). His engraving of *The Battle of the Ten Nudes* (*c*. 1465) was the first to show truly realistic depictions of the male body in action and became the most important and influential image of the fifteenth century. The Florentine sculptor Baccio Bandinelli (*c*. 1493–1560) presented himself to a duke by saying: 'I will show you that I know how to dissect the brain and also living men, as I have dissected dead ones to learn my art.'

The grand masters of art, Leonardo da Vinci and Michelangelo, both conducted anatomical dissections that contributed to their accurate depictions of the human body. Among others who gained knowledge from dissecting bodies were the Florentine sculptor and engraver Domenico del Barbieri (c. 1506–c. 1565) and the Flemish artist Peter Paul Rubens (1577–1640). Both produced images of muscles and bones as they appeared following dissections. Among their contributions

ABOVE: The figures in *The Battle of Ten Nudes*, the only engraving Pollaiuolo ever signed, shows his keen understanding of anatomy.

were Domenico del Barbieri's engraving *Two Flayed Men and Their Skeletons*, made between 1540 and 1545, and Rubens' pen and ink sketch *Anatomical Studies: a Left Forearm in Two Positions and a Right Forearm*, made between 1600 and 1605.

LEONARDO AND ANATOMY

Leonardo began his anatomical studies in 1489 by drawing a skull and dissections he had made on animals, such as a bear and horses. That year he began dissecting human corpses in the Hospital of Santa Maria Nuova in Florence (which still exists). In 1506 he encountered a patient who was 100 years old; after the man died Leonardo was allowed to dissect his corpse, he said, 'to find the cause of such a gentle death'. The result was the first description of coronary heart disease, with Leonardo noting that his death 'came to him through a lack of blood in the arteries that fed the heart and the lower parts which were used up and dried out'.

His opportunities to dissect hard-to-obtain corpses increased when in 1510 he began working with an anatomy professor on several dissections. The anatomist died the following year, and two years later, Leonardo decided to concentrate his research on the human heart. By 1513 he had already dissected some 30 bodies, many by candlelight in the crypt of a church.

More than Michelangelo and others, Leonardo produced deeper probes into the human body and made excellent images of his dissections. He was the first to draw the human spine with its correct curves, and to conduct an accurate anatomical study of a human foetus. After he 'retired' to France in 1516 Leonardo continued his studies of embryology and the valves of the heart, making a glass model of an aorta that used water containing grass seeds to simulate the flow of blood (and since proven to be accurate). Leonardo never published his anatomical drawings or findings, and they were not discovered for almost 400 years.

MICHELANGELO AND ANATOMY

Michelangelo dissected his first bodies at the age of 18, having received permission from the hospital of Florence's Monastery

OPPOSITE: Leonardo's detailed anatomical drawing of a man's neck and shoulders was drawn in about 1510 and included numerous notes.

ABOVE: This dramatic woodcut showing Andreas Vesalius with a dissected body was crafted by the Dutch artist Jan Steven van Kalkar.

of Santo Spirito after he created a wooden crucifix to sit above its altar. The monastery's prior allowed him to use some of the rooms in which to perform dissections (these were illegal at the time, except for dissections of executed criminals).

Michelangelo made sketches of the remains, just as he did after dissecting many types of animals. The Italian artist, architect and historian Giorgio Vasari wrote of Michelangelo in his *Lives of the Most Excellent Painters, Sculptors and Architects*, published in 1550, that: 'In order to be entirely perfect, innumerable times he made anatomical studies, dissecting men's bodies in order to see the principles of the construction of the bones, muscles, veins and nerves, the various movements and all the postures of the human body; and not of men only, but also of animals, and particularly of horses…'

Michelangelo was acknowledged to have performed more human dissections than professional surgeons and to have acquired more knowledge about anatomy, and he continued the dissections into his old age. This understanding contributed greatly to his images of movement, as seen in his slaves and the many bodies in *The Last Judgement*.

As he grew older, however, Michelangelo undertook fewer dissections as the practice began to upset his stomach so badly he found it difficult to eat or drink.

ANDREAS VESALIUS (1514–64)

Vesalius was born in Brussels, now in Belgium but then part of the Holy Roman Empire. From 1529 to 1533 he attended the Catholic University of Leuven, also now in Belgium, then he studied medicine at the University of Paris until 1536. He left when the Holy Roman Empire declared war on France, resuming his medical studies at Leuven and then the University of Padua in Italy, where in 1537 he earned a doctorate and was appointed to lecture in surgery and anatomy.

As a surgeon, Vesalius created anatomical charts for his students. His research involved dissections on corpses, which were difficult to obtain until a judge in Padua began making the bodies of criminals available to him in 1539. His research was in contrast to dissections performed by Galen, the renowned second- century Greek surgeon based in Rome, who only dissected animals such as apes and dogs due to restrictions by the church. Vesalius boldly refuted many of Galen's admired conclusions and in 1543 published *De Humani Corporis Fabrica Libri Septum* (*The Seven Books on the Structure of the Human Body*), the first comprehensive book of anatomy based on his discoveries while dissecting human bodies.

BELOW: Michelangelo's image of the Libyan Sibyl was a preparatory chalk drawing for his monumental figure on the Sistine Chapel ceiling.

That same year he presented the book to Charles V, the Holy Roman Emperor and King of Spain, who appointed him physician to his royal household. When Charles abdicated in 1556, he made Vesalius a count and granted him a lifetime pension. Vesalius was also physician to Charles' son Philip II of Spain, and was the official physician to the Madrid court from 1559 until his death in 1564 on a Greek island on his way back from a visit to the Holy Land.

CHAPTER 4

Exploration

The known world was greatly expanded during the Renaissance by brave voyages of discovery that began in the 1480s. These adventures were driven by the humanistic desire for greater knowledge of distant lands and people, although some voyagers were intent on conquest and plunder.

ONCE THEY began racing to the New World, European explorers had a series of impressive successes: Christopher Columbus landed on the Caribbean islands in 1492; John Cabot reached North America in 1497; Vasco da Gama located a sea route to India in 1498; Ferdinand Magellan's crew completed a voyage around the world in 1522 after his death on a Pacific island; and Francis Drake circled the globe between 1577 and 1580, battling the Spanish along the way. Longer sea voyages led to improvements in ship designs. Hulls became longer and higher, having two or three decks for guns, and sails were increased from three to five.

These dangerous journeys were often made with primitive instruments to determine position and direction. The astrolabe was a disc supposedly used since the second century AD. Sometimes inaccurate, it was used to calculate latitude by

OPPOSITE: Christopher Columbus made landfall on a small Caribbean island on 12 October 1492 and claimed it for Spain's king and queen.

measuring the angle between the horizon and Polaris, the North Star. (One was recovered in 2014 from the wreckage of the *Esmeralda*, one of Vasco da Gama's ships.) By the fourteenth century, the astrolabe began to be replaced by the magnetic compass, which was kept in an open-topped wooden box so that it could be easily read.

Assembling a major expedition was expensive, requiring a fleet of ships outfitted with food and other supplies, as well as a full crew for each vessel.. Financing might come from the crown, as was the case with Columbus, or it might come the explorer's own private funds, like those Vasco da Gama

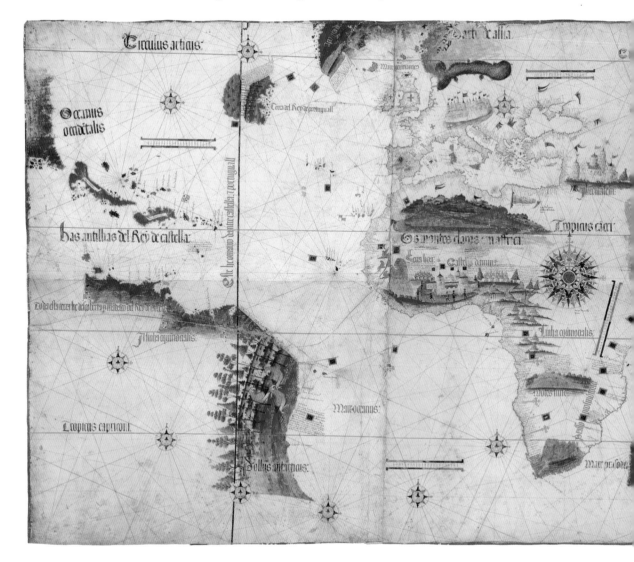

contributed, or by financial investors such as the organization behind England's colony in Roanoke, Virginia.

MAPPING THE WORLD

As Renaissance exploration began, the only known world map was the recently discovered one by the Greco-Roman geographer Ptolemy (*c.* 100 AD–*c.* 170 AD) that was good on ordered space but inaccurate in depicting world geography. This was the accepted map until the new voyages of discovery began to chip away at information about misplaced regions and add new pieces of information. A pioneer who incorporated these changes was

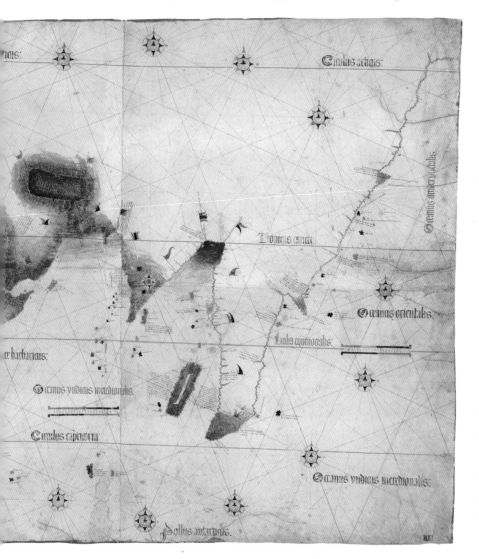

LEFT: The Cantino Planisphere (sphere represented on a plain) was named for the Italian spy Alberto Cantino who acquired it in Portugal.

a German who worked in Florence, Henricus Martellus (dates unknown). His world map, created about 1490, made changes based on the voyage of the Portuguese explorer Bartolomeu Dias (*c.* 1450–1500) between 1487 and 1488 that rounded the Cape of Good Hope. Martellus' map reflected his discoveries by changing the shape of Africa and showing the open water of the Indian Ocean, which Ptolemy had depicted as landlocked.

COLUMBUS RETURNED HOME AS A HERO, STOPPING IN PORTUGAL BEFORE REACHING SPAIN IN TRIUMPH ON 15 MARCH 1493.

Two years after the map was released, Columbus made his western voyage, which would have cartographers at work once more. The *Cantino* world map produced in Portugal in 1502 was the first to add his discoveries, showing the Caribbean islands and parts of Florida and Brazil. This process would see outstanding world maps created by the German cartographers Martin Waldseemüller (1470–1520) and Sebastian Münster (1488–1552) and the Flemish geographer Gerardus Mercator (1512–94).

COLUMBUS (1451–1506)

Christopher Columbus was born Cristoforo Colombo in Genoa, Italy, where his father was a weaver of wool. As a teenager, he went to sea with the Portuguese merchant marines, making several voyages before settling in Portugal. Columbus was certain the Earth was round, so he hoped to find a westward sea passage to the Orient, reaching India, Japan, China and the Spice Islands to take home valuables like silks and spices. He unsuccessfully sought patronage for his plan from King John II of Portugal and, after being rejected twice, Columbus finally won the support of Spain's King Ferdinand and Queen Isabella, who gave him the title of Admiral of the Ocean Sea.

On 3 August 1492, he began the daring voyage with a crew of some 90 men on three ships. The *Niña* and *Pinta* were small caravel ships with triangular sails, while the *Santa Maria* was larger with square sails. It was a difficult journey, and the crew once threatened mutiny if he did not turn back. Columbus promised he would after two more days, but wrote in his journal that he would never have given up. After 10 weeks, on 12 October, they came upon a small island in what later would be named The Bahamas. Columbus named it San Salvador, claiming it for the king and queen of Spain. He called the local inhabitants 'Indians', certain he had found the Indies. On this and later voyages he discovered other islands, including Cuba, first thinking it was 'Cipango' (Japan) and then 'Cathay' (China) and Hispaniola, also thinking it was Japan.

On Christmas Day 1492 his main ship, the *Santa Maria*, struck a rock and foundered. Columbus changed to the *Niña* and left 39 crew members of the *Santa Maria* on the island of Hispaniola (now comprising Haiti and the Dominican Republic) to start a settlement protected by a stockade. He returned home a hero, stopping in Portugal before reaching Spain in triumph on 15 March 1493. He brought with him a few captured natives

BELOW: Columbus bade farewell to Queen Isabella on 3 August 1492 at the Spanish port of Palos de la Frontera.

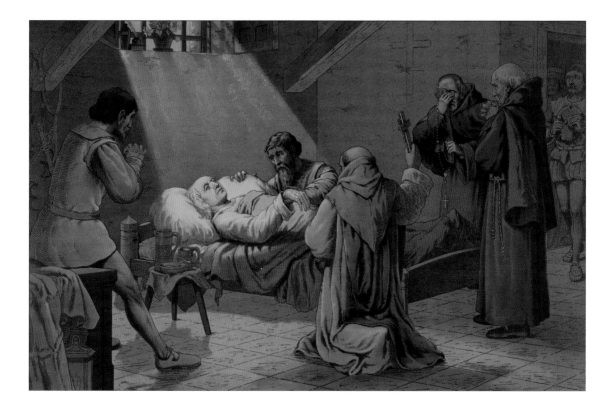

and some gold, along with discoveries including turkeys, parrots, pineapples and spices. He received a big financial reward and the title of Governor of the Indies. A further reward went to Rodrigo de Triana (1469–1535), the sailor who had first spotted the New World from the crow's nest of the *Pinta* (although Columbus had claimed the sighting).

Columbus made three more voyages to the Caribbean, bringing horses with him on the second trip in 1493, which is the first time horses were introduced to the Americas. He still believed it was the Orient. He journeyed to Trinidad and the mainland of South America, then returned to Hispaniola to find the previously friendly local inhabitants had killed the Spanish settlers and destroyed the stockade. Columbus proved to be an inept governor and was accused of mistreating his men and taking brutal revenge on the local inhabitants. This time, when he returned to Spain, he left his brothers Bartholomew and Diego in charge of the settlement. Ferdinand and Isabella of Spain sent a new governor to Hispaniola and had Columbus arrested and stripped him of his titles. He made one more voyage to the Americas, to Panama, still unaware of his more important discovery of a new land and his role in inspiring Europeans to explore, exploit and colonize the Americas.

SWAPPING FOODS

Reaching The Bahamas on his first exploration in 1492, Columbus discovered new exotic foods including maize (corn), squash and pineapples. His crew enjoyed some new tastes but described others as strange or barbaric, such as pudding made from fowl. The natives also served them meals such as *pinole*, made of toasted maize, and *atole*, a hot sweet drink from *masa* or corn flour. Some foods tasted familiar, with Columbus describing a bread that 'tasted exactly as if it were made of chestnuts'.

Explorers in the New World were overwhelmed with the variety of unknown foods. These included new varieties of seafood, maize, beans, squash, turkey, potatoes, sweet potatoes, tomatoes, pumpkins, cassava, peppers, peanuts, pecans, cashews, plantains, blueberries, papaya, avocados and cacao.

For his part, on his second voyage in 1493, Columbus brought back sugar cane from the Canary Islands, off northwestern

LEFT: This document dated 15 May 1492 allowed 'Admiral' Columbus to collect food in Santa Fe, Spain, for his first voyage.

ABOVE: On 7 June 1494,
representatives of Spain
and Portugal signed the
Treaty of Tordesillas at
that town in central Spain.

Africa. It failed to thrive several times before experts were brought in from the Canaries. The first batch of New World sugar cane was shipped back to Europe in 1516. Later voyages introduced old world foods to the local inhabitants, including wheat, oats, barley, rice, radishes, cabbages, lettuce, turnips, vanilla, melons, chickpeas, olive oil and coffee, and livestock such as cattle, chickens, pigs, sheep and goats.

THE POPE DIVIDES THE WORLD

Following Columbus' epic discoveries, European powers were facing the possibility of endless wars to establish New World claims and colonies. Spain and Portugal asked Pope Alexander XVI, who was born in Spain, to resolve this problem, and he responded with a papal bull (a public decree) in 1493 that divided the world into two exclusive spheres by drawing a line north to south through the Atlantic Ocean. Spain was given exclusive rights to lands west of the line, giving them the Americas, and Portugal was given the east and control over Africa and Asia.

Both were given a monopoly on trade in their areas and control of any territory not ruled by a Christian ruler. In practice, this meant ships of other European countries could not sail in either portion and therefore could not establish colonies.

The decision was approved by the two countries in 1494 via the Treaty of Tordesillas in Spain, which moved the line of demarcation further west, giving Portugal the coast of Brazil. Another pope, Julius II, approved the change in 1506. Other European nations immediately disputed the arrangement. Elizabeth I of England said all Europeans had the right to any territory not controlled by a Christian ruler, and Francis I of

A POLITICAL MAP

EVEN THOUGH THEY HAD agreed to divide the New World between them, Spain and Portugal had a bitter dispute over which had rights to the island chain of Moluccas (now part of Indonesia) which were also known as the Spice Islands.

The Portuguese cartographer Diogo Ribeiro (*d.* 1533), who was working for the Spanish Crown, created a world map in 1529 that added information arising from the Magellan crew's circumnavigation of the globe seven years earlier. To help resolve the territorial dispute in Spain's favour, he 'moved' the Moluccas, which belonged to Portugal, just over into Spain's sphere.

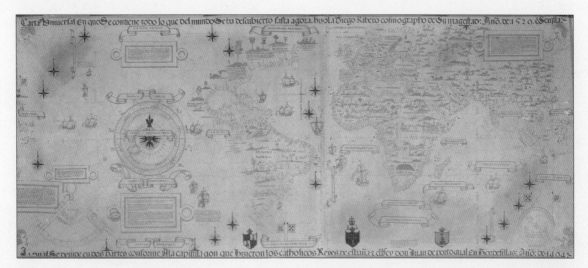

The dividing line Ribeiro put on his map was proven wrong in modern times, but it took centuries to correct.

France said all had to have freedom of the seas. The result was years of conflict, as countries ignored the invisible line.

JOHN CABOT (c. 1450–c. 1498)

Cabot was born Giovanni Caboto, supposedly in Genoa. After hearing of Columbus' discoveries, he settled in Bristol, England around 1490 and later won the support of King Henry VII to sail west to find a route to Asia and the riches of China and Japan (supposedly gold, silks and spices). He left in May 1497 with a crew of 18 on his ship *Matthew* and on 24 June saw land and called it 'New-found land' (now the northern capes of Newfoundland in Canada). Like Columbus, Cabot believed he had reached Asia. After claiming it for England in King Henry's name. he returned home to receive the king's reward of £10 and began planning for a second voyage beyond Newfoundland to discover Japan. This began in May 1498, and this time Cabot took a crew of 300 men in four or five ships with a year of supplies. They never returned, and it was believed he landed in North America but had a misfortune and was unable to return. Another theory

FOODS WERE RATIONED BECAUSE IT WAS UNKNOWN HOW LONG THE TRIP MIGHT TAKE OR IF BAD WEATHER WOULD SLOW PROGRESS.

FOOD PROBLEMS

SUPPLYING FOOD FOR SAILORS on voyages of exploration during the Renaissance was difficult. Often foods were rationed because it was unknown how long the trip might take or if bad weather would slow progress. This minimum amount of food could lead to malnutrition and scurvy from the lack of vitamin C, causing general weakness, loose teeth and often death. The selection of foods also posed a major problem. Although livestock could be taken on board and slaughtered during the voyage, foods like meat and fish had to be smoked, salted or pickled. Cooking with fire on deck posed a danger for wooden ships. Another danger was pests, like rats and mice that would nibble on supplies and leave their droppings, or maggots and weevils that infested foodstuffs.

Common foods included salted meat like pork, fish, hardtack (sea biscuit), hard cheese, beans, garlic and honey. Barrels of beer and wine were carried because fresh water in barrels developed algae.

said he returned to England and died. His voyages, however, inspired a century of English explorations to the Americas. His son, Sebastian (*c.* 1474–*c.* 1557) made several voyages of discovery for England and Spain.

NAMING THE AMERICAS

The achievements of Renaissance explorer Amerigo Vespucci (*c.* 1454 –1512) were recognized by his name being used for three continents of the New World. Born in Florence, he was employed by the powerful Medici family, and his work included fitting out ships for Columbus' second and third voyages. Vespucci became a proficient navigator and was given this position for a Spanish expedition of four ships in 1499 that

discovered the mouth of the Amazon. He believed this was Asia and, returning home the following year, he failed to interest the Spanish in another voyage but found support in Portugal. His second expedition, from 13 May 1501 to 22 July 1502, explored the coast of Brazil, after which Vespucci became convinced this was a 'New World' rather than Asia.

ABOVE: On Vespucci's voyage from 1499 to 1500 as navigator, he is thought to have discovered the mouth of the Amazon River.

In 1507, the German cartographer Martin Waldseemüller published a pamphlet in which he suggested the new land be named after 'Amerigo the discoverer… as if it were the land of Americus or America.' When he and Matthias Ringmann produced the first world map that year, the name was placed only on South America but soon added to North America.

HENRY THE NAVIGATOR (1394–1460)

Although he actually did very little navigating, Henry, Prince of Portugal and Duke of Viseu, who was born in Porto, was the prime early motivator and supporter of Portugal's explorations. These were directed across the Atlantic Ocean and along the

ABOVE: This portrait of Vasco da Gama was produced in 1838 by the Portuguese painter and illustrator Antonio Manuel da Fonseca.

northwest coast of Africa, with the Portuguese being the first Europeans to reach the Cap-Vert peninsula (part of modern-day Senegal). They established colonies in the Azores and Madeira.

Prince Henry's motivation was to establish a sea route to sub-Saharan Africa, where gold and slaves could be taken. This would avoid trade routes run by Muslim rulers since Henry's fervent Catholicism might lead to religious clashes.

VASCO DA GAMA (1460–1524)

Born in Sines, Portugal, the son of a knight and explorer, Da Gama was given command of an expedition in 1497 by the Portuguese crown to find a water route to the east. He left on 8 July 1497 with four ships and a crew of 170 men. They rounded the southern tip of Africa at the Cape of Good Hope on 22 November, and Da Gama then employed an Arab navigator who directed them toward the Indian coast; they arrived in May 1498 at Calicut (now Kozhikode in Kerala, southern India), the first Europeans to sail around Africa to India. The trip home was tragic, with about half the crew dying of scurvy. Nevertheless, Da Gama announced his success to the king, who immediately sent him on another mission with 20 armed ships to display Portugal's might and to open a trading post in Calicut. However, after this was done, locals massacred all those in the trading post, so Da Gama sailed again to India in 1502, attacking Arab Muslim ships along the way. He forced Calicut's ruler to agree to a peace treaty and then established trading posts on the east coast of Africa in what is now Mozambique.

After his return, the king kept him as an adviser on India. In 1524 he was made Portugal's viceroy in India and sent there to handle corruption among authorities. He came down with malaria in Cochin and died on 24 December 1524. His body was returned to Portugal for burial in 1539.

GIOVANNI DA VERRAZZANO (1485–1528)

Born in Tuscany and well educated in Florence, Giovanni da Verrazzano travelled to Egypt and Syria before moving to Dieppe in France in around 1507 to begin a maritime life. He went on several voyages to the Levant (countries on the eastern Mediterranean coast) before securing the support of King Francis I of France in 1523 to find a western route to China. The following January he left in *La Dauphine* with a crew of 50 and two months later reached Cape Fear (now in North Carolina) and sailed north along the American coast. Along the way, Verrazzano kidnapped a local boy to display back in France. On the coast, he discovered the bays that would become those of New York Harbour and Narragansett in Rhode Island. This voyage showed that the eastern coast was continuous from Florida to Cape Breton, Canada. His exploration ended at Newfoundland, and he returned to France on 8 July 1524 to inform the king he had claimed the New World for him.

Verrazzano returned twice to the Americas. In 1527 he led a fleet to Brazil and the next year sailed

BELOW: Because Verrazzano explored the waters around the future New York, the city named the Verrazzano-Narrows Bridge after him.

with his brother Girolamo on two or three ships to trade for spices. They explored Florida, The Bahamas and then the Lesser Antilles in the Caribbean, where he went ashore on the island of Guadeloupe and was captured, killed and eaten by cannibals.

THE CONQUISTADORES

Spanish invaders who explored the Americas and conquered the native civilizations were known as *conquistadores* ('conquerors'). They had a telling advantage, being equipped with armour, cannon and horses unknown to the local inhabitants. Among their most famous leaders were Hernán Cortés (1485–1547), who defeated the Aztecs in Mexico; Francisco Pizarro (c. 1475–1541), who conquered the Inca in Peru; Vasco Nuñez de Balboa (1475–1519), who established the

BELOW: The 1892 lithograph *Entrance of Cortez into Mexico* shows the first meeting of Cortez and Montezuma on 8 November 1519.

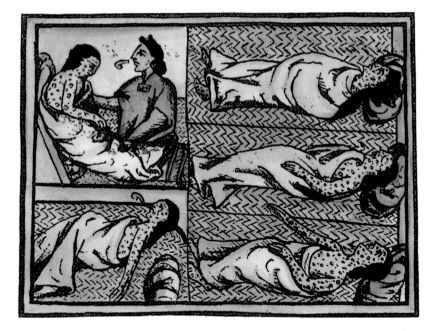

LEFT: A sixteenth-century illustration depicting a medicine man ministering the local inhabitants who had caught smallpox from the Spaniards.

first viable settlement on the continent in Panama and became the first European to see the Pacific Ocean; Juan Ponce de León (*c*. 1460–1521), who named Florida after becoming the first European on the mainland of today's United States; and Hernando de Soto (*c*. 1496–1542), the first European to explore west of the Mississippi River.

The arrival of the *conquistadores* eventually caused the death of more indigenous people by diseases than in battles. Among the most virulent of the old world diseases they brought were smallpox, measles, typhus, diphtheria, mumps and influenza. These epidemics were rapid killers. Four months after the Spanish entered the Aztec capital, disease had taken the lives of about half its population. A century after the European invasion of the American continents, estimates are that diseases killed about 20 million local inhabitants, up to 95 per cent of their population.

Cortés arrived in Mexico with an impressive force in 1519, sailing his fleet from Cuba to the Yucatan Peninsula. The Aztecs believed him to be the god Quetzalcoatl and he easily advanced to their capital Tenochtitlán, where Mexico City is today. The Aztec emperor Montezuma (1466–1520) welcomed them with friendship, but in 1520 Cortés held him as a hostage. Montezuma was supposedly stoned to death by his own people when he tried to quell a rebellion, but some texts believe Cortés murdered him.

Pizarro explored down the west coast of South America. He conquered the Incan empire in 1532, despite being vastly outnumbered. He took their emperor Atahuallpa (*c.* 1502–33) hostage and received a large ransom of gold and silver, but then killed him. The next year he took possession of the capital Cuzco and looted it, before establishing his own city of Lima there in 1535.

JUAN PONCE DE LEÓN (c. 1460–1521)

He was born to a noble family in Santervas de Campos, Spain, and as a boy became the personal attendant to a knight who gave him military training. After fighting in southern Spain against the Muslim Moors, he joined Columbus' second voyage to the New World in 1493 and decided to settle in Hispaniola, marrying and fathering four children. He helped put down native rebellions on the island and in reward was made governor of eastern Hispaniola and given land and slaves.

Restless for more, Ponce de León followed rumours about gold in Borinquen (now Puerto Rico), travelling there secretly in 1506 and discovering some samples. Spain's King Ferdinand gave permission for him to explore the island, which he and a crew did in 1508 and 1509, establishing the first settlement of Caparra.

After hearing more stories about gold and a 'fountain of youth' on an island called Bimini (now part of The Bahamas), he led three ships on the quest in 1513. He reached land that he first thought was Bimini, but it was too large and filled with lush plants. He claimed it for Spain and named it *La Florida* ('The Flowered One') for its beautiful colours and because he had discovered it during Easter, known in Spain as *Pascua Florida*. He

BELOW: Ponce de Leon's 1882 statue in San Juan, Puerto Rico was made from English cannons that attacked there in 1792.

LA HERDIRE ENTERPRINSE FAICT PAR LE SIGNEVR DRAECK AVOIR CIRCVIT TOVTELATERRE

Carte veuee et corige par le dict signeur drack

ABOVE: This world map engraved about 1581 by Nicola van Sype showed Drake's circumnavigation. His route is traced with a dotted line.

...was the first European to land on Florida, on the eastern coast between what today is Saint Augustine and Melbourne Beach. After supposedly failing to locate the fountain of youth (a search that might be a myth) and retreating from a native attack, he sailed past the Florida Keys and up the peninsula's southwest coast to a harbour the Spanish named Carlos and the British renamed Charlotte.

Ponce de León left in 1514 and returned to Spain, where he was knighted and made military governor of Florida and Bimini. In 1521, he sailed for Florida with two ships and a crew of 200 to establish a colony, landing near Carlos Harbour. This prompted a native attack, and Ponce de León was wounded by an arrow and taken to Havana, Cuba, where he died. He was buried there and later reburied in Puerto Rico.

SIR FRANCIS DRAKE (c. 1540–96)

Drake was born in Tavistock in Devon, England, and went to sea at the age of 13. In 1560, he took part in transporting slaves to the New World in a fleet of six ships whose captain was his cousin, John Hawkins. A Spanish squadron attacked and destroyed all but two ships, with Drake and Hawkins escaping

ABOVE: **The arrival of the Spanish Armada in 1588 created an enormous battle scene with 160 Armada ships facing 200 English ones.**

on the *Judith*. This tragedy initiated Drake's lifelong quest for revenge against Spain. After making voyages to the West Indies in 1570 and 1571, he led two ships to attack Spain's Caribbean ports in 1572. Sailing as far as the Pacific Ocean, he captured the port of Nombre de Dios on the Isthmus of Panama. He returned home with Spanish treasures from his raids and attacks on Spanish ships, earning an enhanced reputation as a privateer.

Queen Elizabeth I secretly commissioned him in 1577 to lead an expedition against Spanish colonies along America's Pacific coast. His fleet of five ships sailed that year on 15 November but floundered during the long voyage, and he was left with only his flagship, the *Pelican*, later renamed the *Golden Hind*. He became the first Englishman to navigate through the Straits of Magellan, and he sailed into the Pacific in October 1578. He plundered Spanish ports in South America before sailing north to seek a passage to the Atlantic. When this failed, he turned west and sailed around the Cape of Good Hope for home, arriving on 26 September 1580 with more Spanish treasures and spices, having become the first Englishman to circumnavigate the globe. For this, Elizabeth knighted him aboard the *Golden Hind,* and he was made Mayor of Plymouth in 1581. For their part, the Spanish nicknamed him *El Draque* ('The Dragon').

Drake continued to plunder Spanish settlements, sailing in 1585 to the West Indies and Florida's coast. He stopped to collect colonists on Roanoke Island, off the Carolina coast, who had failed in their attempt to establish the first English colony in the Americas.

In 1587 Drake sailed into the port of Cádiz and destroyed 30 ships being made ready for an invasion of England. When the Spanish Armada did arrive, he was vice admiral of the English fleet that destroyed it in 1588, in large part due to Drake's idea of setting empty ships on fire and sailing them into the Spanish fleet, causing widespread panic. After this success, he made another voyage with John Hawkins to the West Indies that proved a failure when a fever swept through the fleet. He died of dysentery

'THE LOST COLONY'

ENGLAND'S FIRST AMERICAN COLONY was established in 1585 on Roanoke Island, off what was then called Virginia (now North Carolina). It was a venture of Sir Walter Raleigh who had been given the land by Queen Elizabeth. Raleigh gave command of the venture to his cousin Sir Richard Grenville (1542–91), who led the first 107 colonists there, leaving them to return to England for supplies. They built a fort but had constant battles with the local inhabitants. When Sir Francis Drake visited in 1585, his offer to take the settlers with him to England was accepted. A second attempt to establish a colony at Roanoke was made in 1587, when John White (died *c.* 1593) led 115 people to rebuild it. Again, some were killed by the locals and White returned to England for reinforcements, which took three years due to wars with the Spanish. When he landed in Roanoke again, all the colonists had vanished. No sign of fighting was indicated, so he assumed they had moved to another location. They were never found and the settlement became known as 'the Lost Colony'.

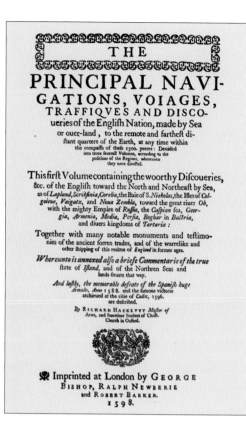

ABOVE: Hakluyt's comprehensive book was part of his promotion of the American colonies. He contemplated a voyage to Virginia but never went.

off the Panama coast on 28 January 1596, a couple of months after his cousin Hawkins had died from the same condition off Puerto Rico. Drake was buried at sea in a lead casket wearing his full armour.

RICHARD HAKLUYT (C. 1552–1616)

While Spain and Portugal were dividing the New World between them, the English geographer and writer Richard Hakluyt was working to inspire his nation to establish colonies. Born in London, he attended Westminster School and Oxford University, reading as much as he could about voyages and discoveries. After graduating in 1577, he began public readings in Oxford about geography.

In 1582 he published *Divers Voyages Touching the Discoverie of America*. The following year he went to Paris as chaplain to the English ambassador to France. While there, he wrote a discourse on western discoveries to prompt English colonization of America, which he presented to Queen Elizabeth I in 1584, the same year he wrote a letter to her secretary of state urging that England immediately lay claim to the American coast before the opportunity would 'waxe colde and fall to the ground'.

After living in France for almost five years, he returned to England and in 1589 published his major work, *The Principal Navigations, Voyages and Discoveries of the English Nation*, expanded to three volumes between 1598 and 1600. He continued to advocate American colonies, especially in Virginia. In 1603 he was elected Archdeacon of Westminster and upon his death was buried in London's Westminster Abbey.

SIR WALTER RALEIGH (C. 1552–1618)

Raleigh was born into a well-connected family in Hayes Barton, Devon, and attended Oxford University without graduating. At the age of 17, he went to France to fight alongside the Protestant

Huguenots in the French wars of religion and returned to study law in London. In 1578 he sailed to America with his half-brother Sir Humphrey Gilbert. Two years later he helped to suppress an uprising in Munster, Ireland, and became the favourite of Queen Elizabeth I. He was given large estates in Ireland and became a member of Parliament in 1584 (where he popularized smoking). The following year he sponsored the establishment of Roanoke colony in Virginia (in present-day North Carolina. At that time 'Virginia' was an area of the American east coast covering parts of present-day Virginia, West Virginia, and North and South Carolina). When it failed, he unsuccessfully tried to re-establish it two years later. In 1585, he was knighted and in 1587 made Captain of the Queen's Guard.

In 1592, the queen discovered that Raleigh had secretly married one of her maids of honour, Elizabeth Throckmorton, and they had an infant son. In a jealous fury, she had the couple locked up in the Tower of London with their baby, who died there. Raleigh's wife was released soon after and Raleigh months later, although he was banished from court for five years. He sought to win back the queen's trust by continuing to write flattering poems about her and then leading an expedition to find El Dorado, the fabled Golden

BELOW: This portrait of Sir Walter Raleigh was painted in 1598 by the English artist William Segar who was knighted in 1616.

Land supposedly in Guiana (now Venezuela); however, this adventure was a failure.

Unfortunately for Raleigh, Elizabeth's successor in 1603 was James I, who had a negative opinion of the reckless explorer and who in 1603 accused Raleigh of plotting against the king. He sentenced Raleigh to death and then reduced this to life imprisonment. Raleigh remained in the Tower of London for 13 years, growing exotic plants, brewing herbal medicines and writing the first volume of his *Historie of the World*, published in 1614. Because of his social status, he was given spacious rooms and could receive visitors.

Raleigh was released in 1616, and the king ordered him to conduct a second search for El Dorado. During the futile voyage, he ignored James' warning not to attack the Spanish and to keep the peace since France was the problem. For this, the king reinstated the death sentence, and Raleigh was beheaded on 29 October 1618.

WHEN THE ENEMY COULD NOT BE FOUND, PRIVATEERS MIGHT TURN INTO PIRATES, ATTACKING ANY SHIP THEY CAME UPON.

BELOW: Columbus said the small caravel *Nina* was his favourite ship, and he used it for all three of his voyages.

SHIPS FOR EXPLORERS

Ships commonly used during the Renaissance included caravels and carracks. Columbus' *Pinta* and *Niña* were caravels, which were smaller and lighter than carracks, having two or three masts and a shallow draught ideal for unknown waters. The caravel, weighing between 50 and 160 tons (50,802–162,568 kg), had a rounded bottom for faster speed, making them popular with pirates who wanted to move quickly.

Carracks, developed by the Spanish and Portuguese, carried two to four masts and had a deeper hull, so they were able to hold more cargo and provisions but were more difficult to manoeuvre. Some weighed up to 2000 tons (2,032094 kg). Explorers favoured them for their stability on the open ocean. Ferdinand Magellan's ship *Victoria*, the first to circumnavigate the world, was a carrack, and Vasco da Gama used three carracks and one caravel for his historic voyage to India. Other examples of carracks were Columbus' *Santa Maria* and Henry VIII's warship, *Mary Rose*.

ABOVE: **The *Golden Hind* was the only one of Drake's five ships to complete his circumnavigation and was retired that year.**

The barque was a combination of the caravel and carrack, having two or three sails. Its smaller size required fewer men to crew it. One, the *Susan Constant*, was used to establish and resupply the English colony at Jamestown – the first permanent English settlement in North America.

A galleon was mainly a warship that carried one or two tiers of guns on its broadside. Having three or four masts, it could be identified by its beaked prow. It had a narrow beam and floor for speed but was made top-heavy by a high poop deck and heavy guns, increasing the danger of capsizing. One example was Francis Drake's *Golden Hind*. The Spanish and Portuguese sailed the largest galleons, mostly for trade and as treasure ships returning home filled with the wealth of the New World. The English made changes under Queen Elizabeth I, to make them faster and easier to manoeuvre.

PIRATES AND PRIVATEERS

The Renaissance saw greater opportunities for piracy. European ships were bringing home treasures from the New World across the Atlantic Ocean, which was too immense for their countries to offer protection or to locate pirates who raided their ships and made swift escapes.

A respectful and even honourable type of piracy existed when sailors were commissioned by a government as 'privateers' to plunder and destroy the ships of a hostile country during war or aggressive overseas competition. During the Elizabethan wars between England and Spain, Spanish galleons were often attacked while bringing riches home from Mexico. Elizabeth I even approved a group of 'Sea Dogs' as raiders and provided them with letters of marque to protect them under English law. Privateers and their crews were normally allowed to keep a portion or all of the takings from ships they had captured. When the enemy could not be found, privateers might turn into pirates, attacking any ship they came upon, regardless of its country.

Among the famed pirates who became privateers were England's Francis Drake and Martin Frobisher. The latter had been arrested many times for piracy in the 1560s but eventually won Elizabeth's respect and was put in command of a squadron during the defeat of the Spanish Armada and eventually earned a knighthood. Another, who received a knighthood and even became an admiral in the navy, was the former pirate Henry Mainwaring.

SIR MARTIN FROBISHER (c. 1535–94)

Born in Yorkshire, England, Frobisher went to sea when he was a teenager and made two voyages in 1553 and 1554 to Africa's Guinea coast. During the latter, he was held hostage by a native chief for several months. He plundered French ships in the English Channel in the 1560s and was arrested at least three times for piracy but released without trials, possibly in return for booty presented to Queen Elizabeth. He was then given command of three ships and on 7 June 1576, with the queen waving farewell, he sailed across the Atlantic to find a northwest passage to the Pacific Ocean. During a great storm near Greenland, one ship was lost, and another returned to England. Frobisher failed to find the passage, but that year he discovered Canada's Labrador and Baffin Island, whose bay Frobisher named for himself.

Back home, he presented a local inhabitant he had captured and won approval for further voyages to the region after

OPPOSITE: This portrait of Frobisher was a seventeenth-century copy of a painting by the Flemish artist Hieronimo Custodis, which was completed about 1590.

ABOVE: A skirmish in 1577 between Frobisher's men and the Inuit was painted by the English artist John White who sailed with Frobisher.

suggesting gold mines were there. He led two more unsuccessful searches, for gold in 1577 with three ships and some 120 men, and in 1578 with 15 ships to discover gold and the passage and to establish a colony. He sailed up the Hudson Strait, which links Hudson Bay with the Labrador Sea, then returned to Baffin Island Bay, where he unsuccessfully tried to establish a colony because the ship carrying timber had sunk. His further search for gold and silver proved futile and royal funding was halted.

In 1585, Frobisher joined Sir Francis Drake's voyage of 25 ships to the West Indies as his vice admiral, a mission that damaged Spanish settlements and yielded the then-enormous sum of £60,000 of booty. In 1588 the two former pirates fought to defeat the Spanish Armada, during which Frobisher was awarded his knighthood. As the battle ended he criticized Drake for sailing near a stricken enemy ship to plunder it. The following year Frobisher and Drake attacked Spanish ships and three years later Frobisher was part of a force sent by Elizabeth to assist France against a Spanish attack. He was fatally wounded in the side during a battle to take a fort in Crozon on the northwest coast of France.

THE 'PIRATE QUEEN'

Grace (Grainne) O'Malley (*c.* 1530–*c.* 1603) was born near Westport in Ireland's County Mayo, the daughter of a clan chieftain who owned a shipping business. At the age of 15, she married a chieftain's son, and they had three children. When her husband was killed during a fight, she inherited his fighting ships and gathered followers together. Soon she married Richard 'Iron Dick' Burke, who owned Rockfleet Castle near Newport in Mayo. She divorced him after one year with her usual force of character, leaning out a window to shout: 'Richard Burke, I dismiss you!' They had one son and remained friends.

Grace now commanded four ships and took to piracy, becoming known as the 'Pirate Queen'. She was known to be fearless and ruthless. She supposedly gave birth to a son aboard her galley shortly before Algerian pirates boarded the ship. Wrapping herself in a blanket, she rallied her crew, and they captured the Algerian vessel. When her husband died, the new English governor began persecuting her family. After two of her sons and a half-brother were captured and imprisoned, Grace sailed up the Thames to request an audience with Queen Elizabeth I of England. This was granted, but Grace refused to bow to Elizabeth because Grace was not her subject. The two

BELOW: A statue of Grace O'Malley by Michael Cooper was unveiled in 2003 in the grounds of Westport House in Westport.

conversed in Latin, and the queen gave the captured men a reprieve and released them. For her part, Grace pledged to end piracy against English ships. She died at Rockfleet Castle and was buried in the Cistercian Abbey on Clare Island in County Mayo.

SLAVERY

Classical texts recovered during the Renaissance justified slavery, with Aristotle believing the master-slave relationship was natural and Thomas Aquinas (later made a Catholic saint) asserting that a slave was the physical instrument of his master, who could claim his slave's children and possessions. This encouraged Renaissance Europeans to enslave indigenous non-Christians for labour. Domestic slavery grew in Florence and other cities following the plague from 1347 to 1348. The Venetians and

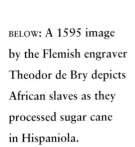

BELOW: A 1595 image by the Flemish engraver Theodor de Bry depicts African slaves as they processed sugar cane in Hispaniola.

TWICE A SLAVE

IN 1518 CHARLES I of Spain authorized slave ships to sail directly from Africa to Spanish possessions, rather than via the usual stop at European ports. Rodrigo Lopez was a slave in Portugal's Cape Verde islands of Africa and received his freedom in his owner's will on his death.

A free man, he was then captured in 1526 by one of his former owner's employees, who kidnapped him at night and forced him onto a ship to Hispaniola (part of Spain's empire) to be sold into slavery again. Lopez, however, was an intelligent man who could read and write Latin. He officially protested his enslavement as illegal because he had been made free, and was once more given his freedom in the early 1530s.

Genoese imported slaves (collectively called Tatars) from Crimea. The Catholic Church saw no need to interfere. In 1488, the Spanish ruler Ferdinand II of Aragon presented 100 Moorish slaves to Pope Innocent VIII, who distributed them among his cardinals and friends.

African slavery began to surge as European countries built their new Atlantic empires. Begun during the Renaissance, this human traffic would last until from 1501 to 1866, with more than 12 million Africans suffering this fate and about two million dying during the voyages. Spain and Portugal first led the slave trade. Spain wanted slaves for plantations in Hispaniola, bringing them in as early as 1501, while Portugal began to transport slaves in around 1545 to work on its sugar plantations in Brazil.

England soon came to dominate in fulfilling the growing demand for slaves from West Indian and North American plantations. This involved capturing or buying local inhabitants on the West African coast and transporting them across the Atlantic. Prominent among slave traders were Sir Francis Drake and his cousin John Hawkins. In 1562 Hawkins made England's first known voyage for African slaves and repeated this twice. He captured more than 12,000 Africans and sold them to Spanish colonies in the Americas.

CHAPTER 5

Literature and Music

The effect of the Renaissance on literature began in the fourteenth century with the influential Dante and lasted into the seventeenth century due to such writers as Shakespeare, Cervantes and Milton. The era also encouraged a new creativity in music, producing great composers like Monteverdi and Thomas Tallis.

THE CREATIVE literature of the early Renaissance suffered from being written in Latin, which had restrictions of form that held back an author's freedom of expression. The introduction of vernacular literature gave language a familiar tone that increased the readership. Dante Alighieri (1265–1321), the Italian poet, writer and philosopher was one of the first to advocate replacing Latin with his native Italian, promoting his 'sweet new style' in *On the Eloquence of the Vulgar Tongue* (*c.* 1304–07) and using the Tuscan language for his masterpiece *The Divine Comedy* (1320). The humanist Petrarch first wrote his poems in Latin but became acquainted with vernacular examples and produced his own, such as the poems of *Rime Sparse* (*Scattered Rhymes*), in Italian. He claimed they were too trivial for him to like, but he carefully collected them. Boccaccio did love the vernacular, which

OPPOSITE: Three young musicians were painted from 1500 to 1540 by an artist, or artists, based in a workshop in Antwerp, Belgium.

he used for his masterpiece, the *Decameron*. English writers also pioneered this change in the fourteenth century, especially the witty Geoffrey Chaucer, who was influenced by Petrarch and Boccaccio and whose *The Canterbury Tales* ranks as one of THE GREATEST narrative poems of all time. Among other outstanding vernacular English poets were William Langland (*c.* 1300–*c.* 1400), whose *Piers Plowman* describes dream visions of ecclesiastical and lay corruption, and John Gower, whose *Confessio amantis* (*Lover's Confession*) provides exemplary tales of love conquering sin.

Writers who composed in their own language also made an impact in other European countries. Sebastian Brant wrote the satirical poem *Das Narrenschiff* (*The Ship of Fools*), which became Germany's most popular work in the fifteenth century. Also popular during that century was the French lyric poet François Villon, best known for his *Le Petit Testament* (*The Little Testament*) and the longer *Le Grand Testament* (*The Great Testament*).

BELOW: Dante's *De Vulgari Eloquentia (Of Vernacular Eloquence)*, written between 1304 and 1307, said the vernacular was a more 'noble' language than Latin.

DANTIS ALIGERII,
PRÆCELLENTISS. POETÆ
DE VVLGARI ELOQVENTIÆ
LIBRI DVO.

Nunc primùm ad vetusti, & vnici scripti
Codicis exemplar editi.

Ex libris Corbinelli:
Eiusdémque Adnotationibus illustrati.

AD HENRICVM,
FRANCIÆ, POLONIÆQV
REGEM CHRISTIANISS.

PARISIIS,
Apud Io. Corbon, via Carmelitarum
ex aduersò coll. Longobard.
1577.
Cum priuilegio.

PETRARCH (1304–74)

He has been called 'the first modern man' and once said: 'I am a citizen of no place, everywhere I am a stranger.' Francesco Petrarca, known as Petrarch, was born in Arezzo, just south of Florence. The son of a merchant and notary, he was forced by his father to study law in 1316 in Montpellier, France. When his father died in 1326, he abandoned law, saying: 'I couldn't face making a merchandise of my mind.' He took up clerical positions that would allow him time to write poetry in both Latin and Italian and travelled through Europe, finding and translating classical Roman literature. On 6 April 1327 in Avignon, France, he became besotted with a woman,

ORso e non furo mai fiumi ne ſtagni :
ne mare ouogni riuo ſi diſgombra :
ne dimuro o dipoggio o di ramo ombra ;
ne nebbia chel ciel copra elmondo bagni :
ne altro impedimento ondio milagni :
qualunche piu lumana uiſta ingombra :
quanto dun uel cheduo begliocchi adombra :
& par che dica or ti conſuma & piagni .
Et quel lor inchinar chogni mie gioia
ſpegne o per humiltate o per argoglio

Laura de Noves, and retained a distant love for her for the rest of his life, writing 366 poems mostly inspired by Laura collected in the book *Rime Sparse*. They included 317 sonnets, a form that Petrarch refined and popularized. Still, he called them 'little triflings' and preferred his epic Latin poem, *Africa*, although that was less popular with readers.

After Petrarch met the poet Giovanni Boccaccio in Florence, the two exchanged letters and writings that formulated their belief in humanism. Petrarch's influence on the Renaissance became widespread when he was crowned poet laureate in Rome on 8 April 1341. In his acceptance speech he praised the classics, saying: 'There was a time, there was an age, that was happier for poets, an age when they were held in the highest honour, first in Greece and then in Italy, and especially when Caesar Augustus

ABOVE: **Petrarch's** *Rime Sparse* *(Scattered Rimes)*, **also called** *Il Canzoniere* *(The Songbook)*, **was a collection of vernacular poems written between 1327 and 1368.**

held imperial sway, under whom there flourished excellent poets: Virgil, Varius, Ovid, Horace and many others.'

From 1351 to 1374 Petrarch wrote *Trionfi (Triumphs)*, combining the classical style with the vernacular voice. In dreamlike visions, it examined the human condition and the triumphs of love, charity, death, fame, time and eternity. He eventually settled in Padua with the immense library he had collected. Petrarch's major influence on English poetry began with Chaucer, who translated his works and composed some similar subjects and thoughts.

OPPOSITE: An illumination of Petrarch's six vernacular poems *Trionfi (Triumphs)* shows 'The Victory of Time over Glory' as humans face heaven.

GIOVANNI BOCCACCIO (1313–75)

Boccaccio was born in Florence, or maybe in the nearby village of Certaldo, the son of a merchant who disapproved of his ambition to write and who, in around 1328, sent his son to study business in Naples. During his time there Boccaccio wrote several poems, including the epic *Teseida* about two friends in love with the same woman. In 1340, he settled in Florence and from about 1348 to 1353 wrote his masterpiece, the *Decameron*, comprising 100 stories from 10 young people who have fled from the plague in Florence for 10 days in a pleasant country villa. In the book, each person is placed in charge of activities for one day and must choose that day's topics for storytelling. The tales range from witty looks at bawdy vices to tragic love stories. The work greatly influenced Renaissance writers and the plots of the tales have often been rewritten and reused in the wider world of literature and storytelling.

England's Geoffrey Chaucer drew more inspiration from Boccaccio than from any other poet. He emulated Boccaccio's style of merging the classical

BELOW: Boccaccio, depicted in this 1833 engraving, used his popular *Decameron* to raise vernacular writing to the standard of classical literature.

form with the vernacular language. Chaucer based his *Troilus and Criseyde* on Boccaccio's *Il Filostrato* and the Knight's Tale in *The Canterbury Tales* on *Teseida*.

In 1350, Boccaccio met Petrarch in Florence, and they quickly built a friendship. The older poet acted as Boccaccio's mentor, and they worked together to establish the ideas for humanism that would inspire the Renaissance. After their association, Boccaccio turned away from vernacular language to write in Latin and concentrated on humanistic scholarship, including a collection of biographies of women written between 1360 and

FAMOUS WOMEN

AFTER THE SUCCESS OF the *Decameron* and affected by the humanism of Petrarch, Boccaccio turned to compiling realistic encyclopedic works in Latin. One of the most popular was the first ever biography of women, *De Claris Mulieribus* (*Concerning Famous Women*). This followed Petrarch writing *De Viris Illustribus* (*On Famous Men*). Boccaccio's work covered the lives of 106 famous and infamous women, and included some mythological figures among the historical ones. Their realistic portrayals influenced Chaucer's characterizations in *The Canterbury Tales*.

Among Boccaccio's selections were: Eve, 'our first mother'; Julia, the daughter of Julius Caesar; Cleopatra, Queen of Egypt; Penelope, the wife of Ulysses; Claudia, a vestal virgin; and Olympia, Queen of Macedonia. While praising the women he selected, Boccaccio said they should be recognized because women have the 'natural' weakness of 'frail bodies and sluggish minds'. He revised and expanded the text during the rest of his life.

Boccaccio collected biographies of famous women, as depicted in this fifteenth-century miniature.

1374. Also, in 1360, Pope Innocent VI ordained Boccaccio as a priest, while the poet was serving as an ambassador at his court.

By 1373, Boccaccio had financial difficulties and was in poor health. Having maintained his admiration of Dante, he wrote a treatise praising the poet and gave public readings of his *Divine Comedy* in Florence. He died two years later in the village of Certaldo, where he had retired.

JOHN GOWER (*c.* 1330–*c.* 1408)

Gower was probably born in Kent, England, to a prosperous family. He apparently practised law in London, where he came to know aristocrats and writers. He became friends with Geoffrey Chaucer, who gave Gower power of attorney when he was sent to Italy on diplomatic business. Chaucer dedicated his *Troilus and Criseyde* to 'moral Gower', and Gower reciprocated in *Confessio amantis*, having Venus praise Chaucer.

In 1398, Gower settled into rooms provided by the Priory of Saint Mary Overie (now Southwark Cathedral) and around 1400 he lost his sight, describing himself as 'old and blind'. Following his death, he was buried in the priory.

Gower's works were written in French, Latin and English. One of his English poems, *In Praise of Peace,* was an appeal to the king to avoid war. His masterpiece, *Confessio amantis,* was in Middle English. It was commissioned by King Richard II, whom Gower met around 1385 on the River Thames. The king invited him onto the royal barge, and their lively conversation resulted in the commission. Gower apparently began writing the poem the next year; it was published in 1390 to great success and with a dedication to Richard II and Chaucer. Several revisions were published, with one in 1392 replacing the original dedications

ABOVE: During his lifetime, Gower's popularity and influence was equal to that of his friend, Chaucer, whose poetry was more vigorous.

with one to Henry of Lancaster, the future King Henry IV. Despite this, no evidence exists to indicate that Gower had turned against Richard II or Chaucer.

Confessio amantis tells of the confessions that Amans (the Lover) makes to Venus' chaplain, Genius. The confession recounts stories that exemplify the seven deadly sins. Gower rewrites stories that were previously known, including those of Ovid, the Bible and some used by Chaucer in *The Canterbury Tales*. After Amans is absolved of his sins, Venus cures him of the unrequited love that had driven him to confess.

CHAUCER BECAME A MEMBER OF PARLIAMENT FOR KENT IN 1386, ALSO SERVING AS A JUSTICE OF THE PEACE.

GEOFFREY CHAUCER (*c.* 1343–1400)

The son of a successful wine merchant, Chaucer was probably born in London. In 1357 he was a page to Elizabeth, Countess of Ulster. Two years later he took part in an expedition of the king's army to Brittany and was captured by the French. King Edward III paid his £16 ransom in 1360 and later sent him on diplomatic missions to France, Genoa and Florence, where he became aware of the works of Dante, Petrarch and Boccaccio.

Around 1366 Chaucer married Philippa Roet, who was a lady-in-waiting to the queen and the sister-in-law of John of Gaunt, the powerful Duke of Lancaster. In 1374 he was appointed Comptroller of Customs for the Port of London on the wool wharf, working there for 12 years as he wrote a body of work that included *Troilus and Criseyde*, a love story set during the legendary Trojan War.

Chaucer became a member of parliament for Kent in 1386, also serving as a justice of the peace. In 1389 he became Clerk of the King's Works, supervising the repair and maintenance of royal buildings such as the Tower of London and Westminster Palace.

Chaucer's first works were *The Book of the Duchess*, written about 1369 to help John of Gaunt overcome the death of his first wife from the plague; *Parlement of Foules*, a playful dream vision of various kinds of love; and *The Legend of Good Women* at the request of Richard II's queen, Anne of Bohemia. He also wrote

OPPOSITE: Chaucer's image appeared on the richly illustrated Ellesmere manuscript of *The Canterbury Tales* created between 1400 and 1410 after his death.

Of gyltes, than ye han herd bifore
Conteyned in this litel tretys heere
To endite with, theffect of my matere
And though I nat the same wordes
As ye han herd, yet to yow alle I prey
Blameth me nat, for as in my contree
Shul ye nowher finden difference
Fro the sentence of this tretys lyte
After the which this murye tale I
And therfore herkneth what that I shal
And lat me tellen al my tale I preye

¶ Explicit

Heere bigynneth Chaucers

A yong man called Mel-
ibeus on his wyf that
which that called was
he for his desport is
his wyf and eek his doghter hath he
the sores seyen faste ysette thre of
and setten laddres to the walles of
been entred and beten his wyf
fyue mortal woundes in fyue sondry
hir feet in hise handes, in hir eyns,
and leften hir for deed and wenten
tornyes was into his hous, and ran
was man rentynge his clothes ya
ye his wyf as ferforth as she dorste
for to styrte, but nat for thy he gan
he woxe ¶ This noble wyf prudente
sentence of Ovide in his book that

¶ Ouidius de remedio amoris

about philosophy and science, including a treatise on how to use an astrolabe to calculate latitude.

In 1387 he began his masterpiece, *The Canterbury Tales*, about a diverse group of 31 pilgrims on their way to Canterbury on horseback who quarrel and pass the time with a storytelling contest, presented with both humour and tragedy. The characters range from a foul-mouthed miller and the carefree wife of Bath to a virtuous knight and a scholarly clerk. Using several literary genres, Chaucer gave them the ease of natural conversation, despite writing within the confines of Middle English. This renowned work was unfinished on his death.

FRANÇOIS VILLON (B. 1431)

Villon was born in Paris as François Montcorbier, but as a young man, he took the surname of the chaplain who became his guardian and tutor when his father died. Villon studied at the University of Paris, receiving a bachelor's degree in 1449 and

THE MILLER

CHAUCER's keen understanding of character is evident in each of the Canterbury pilgrims and can be seen in their descriptions and their stories. They are not one-dimensional stereotypes, but rather individuals with many interests. The miller is a memorable example, presented as a stubby but strong champion wrestler who likes to brawl and even breaks down doors with his head. He is uneducated, foul-mouthed and uncouth, always ready with an obscene story. At the same time, Chaucer points out his better qualities. The miller is a humorous fellow who loves to chatter and has a poetic nature, even composing poems and songs about sinful behavior. As with all the pilgrims, Chaucer describes his flaws and virtues to create a familiar and recognizable character.

This woodcut of the miller from an early edition of *The Canterbury Tales* failed to show his wart and beard.

a master's degree three years later. In 1455 he killed a priest with a sword during a heated argument and was banished from Paris, but in 1456 he received a royal pardon, as the dying priest had forgiven him. Later that year he was involved in a theft from the College de Navarre and again fled the city.

Villon soon wrote a poem he named *Le Lais* (*The Legacy*), but his editors changed the title to *Le Petit Testament* (*The Little Testament*). It involved a series of imaginary bequests to people he left behind in Paris, including ironic choices such as giving his barber clippings from his hair. The poem became his most successful work.

In his subsequent years of travel, Villon was twice arrested and both times released during amnesties. Freed, he produced his longest but less successful poem, *Le Testament*, known later as *Le Grand Testament*, in which he regrets his wasted life and portrays those who received his bequests as having become dissipated. These subjects and those of his shorter poetry reflect the Renaissance's interest in harsh reality; although he was a lyrical poet, Villon also wrote emotional lines about drunks, prostitutes and other examples of suffering humanity.

Villon continued to be arrested during his last years: in 1462 for robbery and the next year for a street brawl. After the latter, he was condemned to be hanged and strangled. As he waited for death, he wrote *Ballade des Pendus* (*The Ballad of Hanged Men*), which describes the bodies of Villon and a few friends hanging after their executions, with gory details of their rotting bodies. However, after an appeal to the French Parlement in January 1463, his death sentence was commuted to banishment for 10 years, and he left Paris to vanish forever.

ABOVE: A 1489 Paris woodcut of Villon whose life of crime and debauchery proved a rich subject matter for his poetry.

SEBASTIAN BRANT (1457–1521)

Brant was born in Strassburg (now Strasbourg, France), the son of an innkeeper. He studied philosophy and law at the University of Basel, earning a bachelor's degree in 1477 and becoming a

Ir gesellen/kumen har noch ze hant
Wir faren jnn schluraffen landt
Vnd gstecken doch jm mŭr/vnd sandt

Doctor griff

Ad Narragoni

Gaudeam omnes

Das schluraffen schiff
Lŭt meyn/vns narren syn alleyn
Wir hant noch brŭder groß/vnd kleyn
Jnn allen landen ŭber al
On end/ist vnser narren zal
t .iiij.

ABOVE: This woodcut appeared in the 1498 edition of Brant's most famous poem published by Johann Bergmann in Basel, Switzerland

doctor of laws in 1489. It was there that he became interested in humanism. He taught law at the university from 1484 to 1500 at the same time as practising law and around 1486 he began teaching literature. He married in 1485 and fathered seven children. Brant returned to Strassburg in 1501 and was appointed its municipal secretary in 1503; Holy Roman Emperor Maximilian I also named him imperial councillor and count palatine (a high palace official).

Brant became noted for his Latin and German poetry. In 1490 he wrote a very popular legal textbook, *Expositiones*. His most successful work was the 1494 long vernacular poem *Das Narrenschiff* (*The Ship of Fools*), a forerunner of the Protestant Reformation, although Brant, a Catholic, later professed indifference to it. His poem was a bitter satire about 110 fools on a ship steered by fools sailing on its way to a fool's paradise, Narragonia. The collection of motley characters included misbehaving clergy, lecherous monks, judges who took bribes, gamblers, adulterers, drunkards, criminals and nosey gossips. Brant was a devoted humanist, and the poem praises knowledge of self as the best type of wisdom. Each chapter was illustrated by a woodcut, many crafted by Albrecht Dürer. The popular work became an immediate bestseller in many countries and was translated into Latin in 1497, French in 1497 and 1498, and English in 1509, 1517 and 1570, as well as into Dutch and other languages.

ELIZABETHAN AND JACOBEAN DRAMA

Renaissance literature split into the Elizabethan era in England to produce some of the world's greatest writers. Foremost was William Shakespeare, whose insightful and imaginative dramas included comedies, histories and tragedies. Among his best-known works are *Hamlet*, *King Lear*, *Macbeth*, *Romeo and Juliet*, *Othello* and *A Midsummer Night's Dream*.

Other renowned Elizabethan writers included Christopher Marlowe, who established blank verse in works such as *Tamburlaine the Great* and *The Tragicall History of Dr Faustus*; Edmund Spenser (*c.* 1552–99), who produced the great poem *The Faerie Queene*, consisting of six books about the adventures of knights; and Sir Philip Sidney (1554–86), who wrote famous sonnets and *The Defence of Poesie*, an essay that introduced a critical analysis of imaginative literature, praising its role as a teacher.

During the reign of Elizabeth's successor James I, who ruled in England from 1603 to 1625, the theatre-going public began to demand more realistic depictions of society. Playwrights answered with dramas of moral corruption that looked at the dark side of Renaissance desires, such as human ambition and selfishness. This led to an increase in extreme violence and sex on the stage. Shakespeare created more personal villains like the psychopath Iago in *Othello*, who eventually causes Othello to strangle Desdemona. John Webster (*c.* 1580–*c.*1632) contributed more violence in the name of ambition in *The White Devil* and *The Duchess of Malfi*. Personal

BELOW: The illustrated title page for Edmund Spenser's long poem published in 1590. An expanded second edition appeared in 1596.

THE FAERIE QVEENE.

Difpofed into twelue books,

Fafhioning

XII. Morall vertues.

LONDON
Printed for William Ponfonbie.
1590.

revenge was the subject of *The Atheist's Tragedie Or the Honest Man's Revenge* by Cyril Tourneur (*c*.1575–1626). Ben Jonson, on the other hand, provided comic relief for audiences through works such as the popular *Every Man in His Humour*.

CHRISTOPHER MARLOWE (1564–93)

A trailblazer of Elizabethan drama (although he only wrote four major plays) Marlowe was born in Canterbury, the son of a prosperous shoemaker. Also called 'Kit' Marlowe, he studied there at the King's School and then won a scholarship to Cambridge University's Corpus Christi College, where he received a bachelor of arts degree in 1584. A master's degree was awarded in 1587 despite his long absences from the college, and it required intervention from the Privy Council of the Queen. This said Marlowe had been on 'matters touching the benefit of his country', the first indication that he may have been a secret agent for the intelligence service.

A writer of tragedies, he was the first English dramatist to demonstrate the appeal of blank verse poetry. His first play *Tamburlaine the Great* in 1587 was also one of the first in blank verse and won him high acclaim. It told of a powerful and cruel but tragic hero who could not defeat a fatal illness. In around 1590 Marlowe created another hero hungry for power, the wealthy Jewish merchant Barabas in *The Famous Tragedy of the Jew of Malta*. Marlowe's most renowned play was *The Tragicall History of Dr Faustus*, a 1592 morality play in which the doctor sells his soul to the devil to acquire knowledge and power. In the *Massacre of St Bartholomew's Day,* written in 1593, he dramatized the real-life slaughter of Protestant Huguenots by Catholics in Paris in 1572.

In 1593 Marlowe's former housemate Thomas Kyd was arrested for posting 'lewd and mutinous lies' around London. When his rooms were searched, a document was found denying the deity of Jesus Christ. Under torture, Kyd said it belonged to Marlowe, who was then told to appear before the Privy Council. Before he could appear on 30 May, he got into a row with four men in a tavern in Deptford in southeast London, supposedly

OPPOSITE: **This 1585 portrait, believed to be that of Christopher Marlowe, was discovered in 1952 at Corpus Christi College, Cambridge University.**

ANNO. DÑI   ÆTATIS SVÆ 21
1585

QVOD ME NVTRIT
ME DESTRVIT

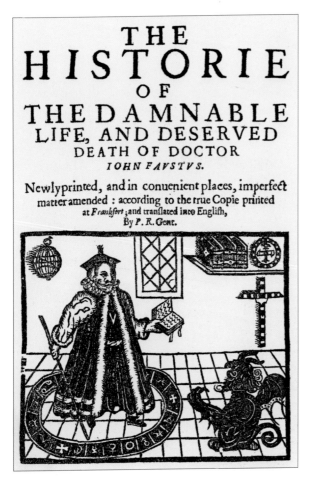

THE
HISTORIE
OF
THE DAMNABLE
LIFE, AND DESERVED
DEATH OF DOCTOR
IOHN FAVSTVS.

Newly printed, and in conuenient places, imperfect
matter amended : according to the true Copie printed
at *Frankfort* ; and translated into English,
By P. R. *Gent.*

ABOVE: Publications
began in the 1580s about
the German alchemist,
astrologer and magician
Doctor John Faustus
whom Marlowe used
for his play.

OPPOSITE: The Cobbe
portrait, supposedly the
only one of Shakespeare
during his lifetime, has
been in the Cobbe family
for some 300 years.

about a bill, and he was fatally stabbed
in the eye by a man named Ingram Frizer.
Marlowe was buried in an unmarked
grave in the churchyard of St Nicholas
Church in Deptford. One conspiracy
theory claimed he had been murdered
by members of the Privy Council after
Marlowe, a secret atheist, had discovered
that four Council members were also
atheists, a heresy that could lead to
their executions.

WILLIAM SHAKESPEARE (1564–1616)

The son of a prosperous glover, tanner
and wool dealer, Shakespeare was born
in Stratford-upon-Avon in Warwickshire,
the oldest of eight children. He attended
local schools, where he learned Latin and
Greek and read the classical literature
from which he would later take plots and
characters for his plays. He left school
at age 14 or 15 and in 1582 at age 18 he
married Anne Hathaway, who was 26,
and they had three children. Little is known about his activities
between 1585 and 1592, known as his 'lost years' before he was
known to be living in London in 1592.

An outbreak of plague forced London's theatres to close
between 1592 and 1594, so Shakespeare began writing poetry,
including sonnets and the erotic poems *Venus and Adonis* and
The Rape of Lucrece. Among his early plays were the three
parts of *Henry VI, The Two Gentlemen of Verona* and *Titus
Andronicus.* In 1594 he became a founding member of the
Lord Chamberlain's Men, in which he was a playwright,
actor and shareholder.

Rival playwrights made an effort to injure Shakespeare's
reputation, with Robert Greene calling him 'an upstart crow', but
his growing fame had his name first appearing on the title page

of *Love's Labour's Lost* in 1598. The following year his company moved to the Globe theatre, which they had built south of the Thames. It was an open-air amphitheatre of three storeys under a thatched roof with a capacity of 3000. It had standing space in front of the stage for poor people who could not afford seats, and these 'groundlings' were often rowdy and hurled abuse at the actors.

RIVAL PLAYWRIGHTS TRIED TO INJURE SHAKEPEARE'S REPUTATION, WITH ROBERT GREENE CALLING HIM AN 'UPSTART CROW'.

Shakespeare's troupe also often performed before Queen Elizabeth, and when she died in 1603 and James I assumed the throne, he changed the company's name to The King's Men. They continued to give frequent performances at the royal court and in 1608 acquired a second venue, the indoor, candlelit Blackfriars Theatre.

Responding to the public's desire for darker plots in the Jacobean years, Shakespeare wrote *Othello*, *King Lear* and *Macbeth* (which has a sympathetic portrayal of King James' ancestor, Banquo). Among his last plays were romances that were grave in tone but were less tragic: *Cymbeline*, *The Winter's Tale* and *The Tempest*.

During the Elizabethan and Jacobean era, from 1590 until his retirement in 1613, Shakespeare wrote 37 plays that included 17 comedies and 9 histories, along with 154 sonnets and four other poems. His plays introduced some 300 new words and many phrases we still use today. His successful career won him the name of 'the

Bard' and made him wealthy. He purchased several substantial properties in Stratford, including the town's second-largest house, New Place, in 1597.

The Globe burned to the ground in 1613, apparently when a cannon misfired during a performance of *Henry VIII*, which Shakespeare wrote with John Fletcher (1579–1625). That same year Shakespeare retired after writing his last play, *The Two Noble Kinsmen*, another collaboration with Fletcher. He died at the age of 52 on 23 April (supposedly his birthday) in 1616 and was buried in the sanctuary of Holy Trinity Church in Stratford. His widow Anne died in 1623 and was buried beside him. By then, 18 of his plays had appeared in cheap quarto pamphlets, and in 1623 two actors from his company had 36 plays published in the First Folio that sold for £1. In its preface, Ben Jonson wrote: 'He was not of an age, but for all time.'

BELOW: This vintage illustration shows Shakespeare and his Lord Chamberlain's Company performing for Queen Elizabeth I in 1594 at Greenwich Palace.

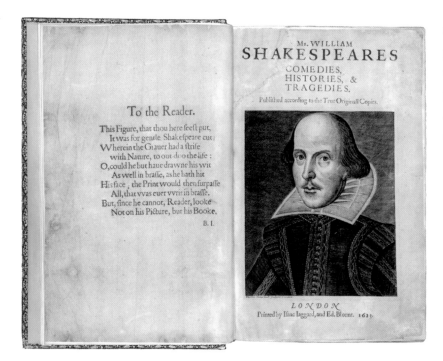

The illustrated title page of the First Folio of Shakespeare's works published in 1623. Martin Droeshout engraved the portrait.

BEN JONSON (1572–1637)

Benjamin Jonson attended Westminster School in London in the late 1570s, developing a love for classical authors like Horace. He would later write of his tutor, the famed historian William Camden, crediting him as being responsible for 'All that I am in arts, all that I know.' Before concentrating on writing, Jonson served as a soldier in the Netherlands and worked for his stepfather, a bricklayer. He married in 1594 and fathered a son and a daughter, both of whom died young.

Jonson began acting in London, before turning to playwriting in 1597, when his first known play, *The Case is Altered*, was performed. A year later saw his great success, the sophisticated comedy *Every Man in his Humour*. Among his string of popular comedies were *Volpone* (1606), *The Alchemist* (1610) and *Bartholomew Fair* (1614). His work was especially enjoyed by James I, who rewarded him with a royal pension and encouraged him to write new comedies for the royal family. Jonson also wrote masques of songs and dance for both James I and Charles I, with Inigo Jones designing the sets before tensions broke up their collaborations.

THE RENAISSANCE OF THE GLOBE

After the Globe burned down in 1613, it was rebuilt the following year. The Puritan government banned all theatres from opening in 1642, so the Globe was turned into tenement housing. Its modern rebirth was due to the sustained efforts of the American actor and director Sam Wanamaker, who moved to England in 1950. He supervised the rebuilding of the Globe as close to the original as possible. In 1989 the buried foundations of the original building were discovered, leading to adjustments to the planned design. The new Globe opened in 1997 near the old site, with space for 1400. The Sam Wanamaker Playhouse opened next to it in 2014, a covered candlelit theatre in the style of the Blackfriars Theatre, with a capacity of 340.

The new Globe Theatre founded by Sam Wanamaker which, after several years of planning, opened in 1997.

In 1616 Jonson published *Workes*, a collection of his plays and poetry. That year James I also named him as England's first poet laureate (without that title) and added a pension. After Shakespeare's death, Jonson was considered by many to be England's greatest living writer. This opinion was not held by all of his rival playwrights, some of whom disparaged his quarrelsome and pompous nature. Even his friend, the Scottish poet William Drummond, described him as 'a great lover and praiser of himself, a condemner and scorner of others…' In 1598 Jonson had killed a man during a duel and was almost executed for manslaughter, avoiding death by 'benefit of clergy' (his ability to read from the Latin Bible). About three years later he took revenge on his critical rivals by attacking them in his satirical play, *Poetaster*.

Despite being overweight and having a reputation for drunkenness, Jonson walked to Scotland in 1618 to visit Drummond. In 1628, he was made the chronologer for the City of London, but that year he died in near poverty and was interred in Westminster Abbey, the only person buried there in an upright position. He supposedly told the dean of the abbey that he could not pay for more space for his body.

BELOW: Prior to becoming a master of comedy, Ben Jonson wrote tragedies. He was also an esteemed literary critic.

MUSIC

The Renaissance-inspired new ways of composing music, produced works that were diverse and exhilarating. For the first time, voices were blended with instruments in a polyphonic structure familiar to western audiences today. Humanists read ancient Greek ideas about music's power to stir the emotions, and this led to works like the dramatic Spanish madrigal and the new genre of opera. The best music in the early Renaissance was reserved for churches, but by the late sixteenth century composers had responded to the desires of a wider audience, from royal courts to wealthy individuals. In the fifteenth century, the English composer John Dunstable greatly influenced European composers with his sweet melodic works. The Burgundian court in the Netherlands was the focal point for innovative composing during the fifteenth century, patronizing the famed French composer Guillaume Du Fay, who introduced Dunstable's melodic lyricism around French poetry, mostly for church masses. Around this time a more complex international European style was developed in France by Josquin des Prez, who also used French poetry and popular songs. The Protestant Reformation and later Catholic Counter-Reformation in the sixteenth century led to simpler hymns and clear lines. The English composer William Byrd, who was a Catholic, managed to survive composing for the Catholic Church and Protestant Queen Elizabeth I.

DUNSTABLE GREATLY INFLUENCED EUROPEAN COMPOSERS WITH HIS 'ENGLISH MANNER' COMPOSITIONS, FEATURING FLOWING AND SONOUROUS HARMONIES.

BELOW: The musical score for the three-part madrigal, *Pastime with Good Company*, said to have been written by Henry VIII.

New musical instruments were also introduced. The violin appeared, promoted by Catherine de' Medici, the powerful queen consort and later Regent of France, and its dramatic tones would soon see its popularity overshadow that of the viol. Other new instruments included the sackbut, an early type of trombone, and the shawm, a predecessor of the oboe.

The first music books were printed in 1501 by the Venetian printer Ottaviano dei Petrucci (1466–1539). Their distribution around Europe broke the exclusive ownership by the church and rich of hand-written music books.

JOHN DUNSTABLE
(*c.* 1385–1453)

The Englishman who led the way into early Renaissance music, Dunstable greatly influenced European composers with his 'English manner' compositions, featuring flowing and sonorous harmonies. He was recognized as the most celebrated English composer of the fifteenth century.

Dunstable served the Duke of Bedford, who was regent of France from 1422 to 1435. They travelled there together and visited the courts of France, which made Dunstable's sweet music popular. It enriched the harmony of compositions around the European continent, which were stark and dissonant. His works included sections of church masses, motets (polyphonic vocal compositions) and secular songs. His cyclic masses had each section built over a single tenor and were innovative works that became the standard for mass compositions for a century. Dunstable might have invented the motet with a double structure using the two melodies of a pre-existent plainchant *cantus firmus* (or 'fixed song' in Latin) in the tenor and a melody in the treble with variations.

He left around 60 compositions, almost all of which are sacred. He was also knowledgeable in mathematics and astronomy. He died on 24 December 1453 and was buried in the church of St Stephen Walbrook in the City of London. Dunstable's tombstone and the church, which contained a memorial to him, were destroyed in the Great Fire of 1666.

ABOVE: John Dunstable spread out the pitches of different singers, instead of following the Middle Ages' idea of same-pitched harmony.

ABOVE: The score depicted is for one of Du Fay's compositions. They provided a link between late medieval and Renaissance music.

GUILLAUME DU FAY
(1397–1474)

Born in Beersel near Brussels in the Netherlands (now in Belgium), Du Fay, also spelt Dufay, was in 1409 a chorister in the cathedral of Cambrai (now in France). His musical talents were praised when young; he travelled to Italy and in 1420 served the influential Carlo Malatesta in Rimini, then went to Rome and in 1428 joined the papal choir. In 1436 he returned to Cambrai to become a canon, and by around 1440 he was supervising the cathedral's music. In 1446, he became a canon in Sante-Waudru in Mons (now in Belgium). He made numerous journeys between Cambrai and Italy, once travelling to Savoy in 1452 and remaining in Italy for six years, during which time his many compositions included a lamentation on the fall of Constantinople in 1453.

Du Fay was universally regarded in the fifteenth century as the greatest composer of his era. His surviving compositions include 87 motets and 59 French chansons. He wrote motets for several celebrations, including the consecration of Brunelleschi's Dome for Florence Cathedral in 1436. Du Fay's graceful music for church masses in four voices included sacred melodies and secular songs that would inspire the development of musical masses. For these, he adopted the sweet harmonies of John Dunstable to recreate the *contenance angloise* ('the English manner'). His secular songs, mostly for three voices, used the three *formes fixes* ('fixed forms') combining French verse with the music: the rondeau (especially for love songs); ballade; and the virelai, composed around short French verses. Du Fay's reputation throughout Europe was largely based on his perfect control of these forms.

JOHANNES OCKEGHEM (*c.* 1410–97)

Ockeghem (also known as Jean de Ockeghem) was born in Saint-Ghislain, Belgium. Known for his beautiful voice, he sang as a chorister in Antwerp Cathedral from 1443 to 1444 and then at Moulins in the chapel of Charles, the Duke of Bourbon, from 1446 to 1448. He spent most of his career working in the French royal court, becoming the composer and chaplain to three successive French kings: Charles VII, Louis XI and Charles VIII. He also served as treasurer of the Abbey of Saint-Martin in Tours. Ockeghem's extensive travels around Europe made him familiar with the various styles of music that he used in his own compositions and for teaching many future composers.

BELOW: This 1537 engraving shows Ockeghem (third from left, wearing tinted glasses) at the lecture with men singing from large music sheets.

Ockeghem wrote at least 13 cyclic masses, some in freestyle and some in *cantus firmus*. He was also known for his motets and secular works. He gained European fame in 1460 with a motet chanson, *Mort, tu as navré* (*Death, You Have Wounded*), at the death of a close friend. Ockeghem was expert with counterpoint and a master of the 'canon technique', in which the initial melody is repeated later, either in the same pitch or in different ones. He used this for mass compositions such as *Missa prolationum* (*Prolation Mass*) (*Pope Marcellus Mass*) for four voices and consisting of two canons proceeding together at different speeds.

WILLIAM BYRD (*c.* 1538–1623)

Born in London, he became a renowned composer and organist during the Elizabethan period. He was a pupil of Thomas Tallis (*c.* 1505–85), also a famous composer and organist, and in 1572 the two men shared the position of organist for the Chapel Royal. In 1575 Queen Elizabeth I gave them a monopoly to print and publish music and music paper, and in that year their first publication was a collection of 34 motets dedicated to Elizabeth. A Catholic, Byrd had thrived under the Catholic Queen Mary I but remained in good favour with the Protestant Elizabeth I and James I, her successor. This encouraged him to publish two books of *Gradualia* (music for major Catholic feasts) in 1605 and 1607 that contained the most music for Roman masses ever produced

VIRGINALS AND SPINETS

ONE OF THE MOST popular musical instruments of the Renaissance was the virginal, possibly the earliest form of a harpsichord. Both have strings that are plucked, but unlike the harpsichord's vertical strings, the virginal's strings are horizontal in a rectangular case (sometimes hexagonal in Italy) and plucked by keys, like a piano. A related instrument is the spinet, which is wing shaped. Both resemble small pianos, but the virginal's strings run almost parallel to the keyboard, while the spinet's are at an oblique angle. A variation is the spinet virginal, which has its keyboard projecting up instead of being inset.

Elizabeth's I virginal is in London's Victoria & Albert Museum. It was made in 1594 in Venice.

The virginal's sound is crisp and light and remains the same whatever force is applied to the keys. It was ideal for Renaissance polyphonic compositions for many voices because the player could produce more than one melody at the same time. Elizabeth I owned one and was known to be an accomplished player.

by a composer. This was particularly daring, following the 1605 Gunpowder Plot by Catholics against King James.

Tallis died in 1585 and Byrd began publishing collections of his own compositions, including *Psalmes, Sonets and Songs of Sadness and Pietie* in 1588. Many of his church compositions were sung in English. His keyboard style for organ and virginal music set a new high standard, and he developed the free form of the fantasia that became a mainstay in Jacobean music.

THE ACCESSION OF JAMES I IN 1603 INSPIRED BYRD TO PUBLISH MORE OF HIS COLLECTIONS OF MUSIC FOR MASSES.

In 1593 he moved from Harlington, Middlesex, where he had lived since 1577, to Stondon Massey in Essex, and remained there for the rest of his life. The accession of James I in 1603 inspired Byrd to publish more of his collections of music for masses. In 1611 his last publication was of the new *Psalmes, Songs and Sonnets* comprising sacred and secular music.

JOSQUIN DES PREZ (c. 1450–1521)

The French-Flemish composer was born in Hainaut on the French-Belgian border (now in Belgium) and by the 1470s he was singing with the choir in the cathedral of Cambrai, France. He later performed in several courts, including the Chapel Royal of France's King Louis XII. Around 1476 he wrote a famous motet, *Ave Maria, virgo* Serena (Ave Maria, serene virgin). In 1489 he went to Rome to serve in the pope's chapel, writing music and remaining there until 1495. He later became choirmaster for Duke Ercole I of Ferrara, for whom he wrote a mass, *Hercules Dux Ferrariae* (Hercules Leader Ferrara), and the motet, *Miserere* (Have Mercy). When the duke died in 1505, Josquin went to Condé as provost of the church of Notre Dame.

His compositions were praised by Martin Luther, who said Josquin was 'master of the notes, which must do as he wishes; other composers must do as the notes wish'. Much of his popularity came from introducing the modern style of tonality and expressiveness that was then unknown in sacred music. For his secular chansons, Josquin used a freer form of counterpoint

ABOVE: Shown is the title page of Willaert's *Musica Nova* (*New Music*), a collection of motets and madrigals published in 1559.

for five or six voices. One of his most popular songs, written around 1498, was the humorous *El Grillo* (*The Cricket*) for four voices, imitating the sound of a cricket singing in the grass.

ADRIAN WILLAERT (*c.* 1490–1562)

Probably born in Bruges, Belgium, Willaert went to Paris to study law but soon changed to pursue music and studied with Jean Mouton, the chief composer for the French Chapel Royal. In 1515 Willaert was in the service of Cardinal Ippolito I d'Este of Ferrara and, on his death in 1520, served Duke Alfonso d'Este of Ferrara. In 1525 he took the same position with Ippolito II d'Este in Milan. His fame became secure with an appointment in 1527 as *maestro di cappella* (director of music) of St Mark's in Venice. He continued in this position until his death and, as his reputation spread, musicians across Europe travelled to study under him. He founded the Venetian School, which anticipated Baroque music's emotional intensity under composers like Bach and Handel. This made Willaert the most influential composer between the death of Josquin des Prez and the rise of Palestrina. He left eight masses, more than 150 motets and many Italian madrigals, French chansons, hymns and psalms. He refined the madrigal with the contrapuntal style and was one of the first to write strictly instrumental works.

Willaert supposedly invented the antiphonal style of music performed by two interacting choirs, and this evolved into the Venetian School's polychoral music. He composed many works for the choirs and in 1550 published *Salmi spezzati* (*Broken Psalms*), polychoral music for the psalms.

GIOVANNI PIERLUIGI DA PALESTRINA (*c.* 1525–94)

He was born in Palestrina near Rome and used to sing as he sold his family's farm produce in Rome's streets. At the age of 12, Palestrina was supposedly heard by the choirmaster of the

basilica of Santa Maria Maggiore in Rome, who took him into
its choir and taught him music. From 1544 to 1551 he was the
organist for the cathedral of St Agapitus in Palestrina and in
1551 became *maestro* for the papal choir in St Peter's Basilica.
Pope Julius III made him musical director of the Julian Chapel
after seeing Palestrina's first publication of music for masses. He
took other appointments to chapels in Rome and returned to
the Julian Chapel in 1571. After the plague killed his wife, two
sons and brother, Palestrina married a rich widow who provided
financial security for the remainder of his life.

Palestrina composed mostly masses and motets, but also
madrigals. He was the most successful Italian composer in
assimilating the new smooth polyphonic techniques of the
Franco-Flemish composers, being especially influenced by Josquin
des Prez. He was known for following his own strict rules of

LEFT: A contemporary
woodcut showing
Palestrina in 1554
presenting his first
book of masses to Pope
Julius III, to whom it
was dedicated.

composition, including a dynamic flow of music and keeping the melody from making leaps between notes. He was called the perfect composer and the ideal one for Catholic music, because he could write sweet, modern music that was acceptable to the strict demands of the church. He lived through 13 popes and the Catholic Church's Counter-Reformation, which raised questions about the style of sacred music. Palestrina overcame the doubts by writing purely beautiful music, and he has been called 'the saviour of church music'. His most famous mass composition, *Missa Papae Marcelli* (Pope Marcellus Mass*)*, is still sung regularly in Catholic churches.

ORLANDE DE LASSUS (c. 1532–94)

He was born in Mons, Belgium, and at eight years old sang there in the choir of St Nicolas' church. Ferdinand of Gonzaga, a general of the Holy Roman Emperor Charles V, took him into service and, after a campaign in the Netherlands, Lassus (also spelt Lasso) accompanied him to Italy in 1544, remaining for nearly a decade in Milan, Sicily and Naples. He went to Rome in 1553 to serve a year as chapel master of the papal church St John Lateran. In 1556 he settled permanently in Munich as

MUSIC PUBLISHING

THE MAN MOST RESPONSIBLE for spreading Renaissance music in the fifteenth and sixteenth centuries was Ottaviano dei Petrucci (1466–1539), an Italian printer who produced 61 music publications, mostly of masses, motets, chansons and frottole (popular, non-religious songs). He was born in Fossombrone in central Italy and in 1490 he moved to Venice, where he was given a monopoly to print music from 1498 to 1511. In 1501, he was the first person to use movable type to print polyphonic compositions in a collection of about 100 chansons, *Harmonice Musices Odhecaton (One Hundred Songs of Harmonic Music)*. He also printed the first lute music in 1507. His printing process required three separate imprints for the music's staff, notes and text. Among the renowned composers whose works he printed were Josquin des Prez and Johannes Ockeghem. Because Petrucci selected Franco-Flemish music, that style quickly became the most popular in Europe.

ABOVE: Monteverdi's portrait was painted during his lifetime by the Genoese artist Bernardo Strozzi. They came together after they both moved to Venice.

director of the court chapel of Duke Albrecht V of Bavaria and then under his son and successor, William V. Emperor Maximilian raised him to the nobility in 1570 and Pope Gregory XIII made him a knight of the Golden Spur after Lassus dedicated a collection of masses to him in 1574. In the 1590s his health began to fail, and on the day he died William V decided to dismiss him to save money, but Lassus never saw the letter.

Lassus composed more than 2000 works and was a master of both sacred and secular music. His most popular collection was in 1584 of seven sombre penitential psalms, *Psalmi Davidis Poenitentiales* (*Penitential Psalms of David*). These so impressed Duke Albrecht that he had them written on parchment and beautifully illustrated by an artist. Lassus was ahead of other composers in his universal use of music from several nations. He became the leading composer of Italian madrigals (with a collection published in 1555), motets (with his first collection in 1556) and of French chansons in 1570. He also published seven collections of German lieder (songs usually composed for a single voice with keyboard accompaniment).

CLAUDIO MONTEVERDI (1567–1643)

Monteverdi was born in the northern Italian town of Cremona to a barber-surgeon and studied under the director of music for the town's cathedral. He published two collections of madrigals in 1587 and 1590 and also around 1590 he became a violin player for the Duke of Mantua and published another book of madrigals. He joined the duke's travels to Hungary in 1595 and

Flanders in 1599. Three years later he was named *maestro di cappella* (director of music) for the duke.

Monteverdi published two more books of brilliant madrigals in 1603 and 1605. The latter de-emphasized strict contrapuntal style while adding dissonance and drama to the music. Replying to criticism of his dissonant style, he said: 'My point of view is justified by the satisfaction it gives to both the ear and to the intelligence.' In 1610 he published his celebrated *Vespers* church music, which combined many styles, including instrumental and operatic music. He moved in 1613 to Venice, where he became *maestro di cappella* for St Mark's Basilica.

Monteverdi's music bridged the late Renaissance and early Baroque eras. He played a major role in developing the new genre of opera. He wrote 10 operas, of which the music of seven have been lost. His first was *L'Orfeo* (*Orpheus*), commissioned by Prince Francesco Gonzaga for the 1607 carnival season. Called 'a musical tale', it dramatically combined music, including madrigals and lute songs, with theatrical effects. The following year he published *L'Arianna* to great success but did not write another opera until 1627. The first opera house opened in Venice in 1637 and *L'Arianna* was revised as the first performance. In 1638 Monteverdi published his eighth book of madrigals, *Madrigali Guerrieri et Amorosi* (*Madrigals of Love and War*), in which he represented war by an agitated style for the strings, including striking them with the wood of the bow. Monteverdi continued to publish into his 70s, with three operas and, in 1640, an impressive collection of sacred music, *Selva Morale e Spiritual* (*Moral and Spiritual Forest*).

BELOW: This very rare manuscript was handwritten by Monteverdi and discovered in the archives of a church in Mdina, Malta.

CHAPTER 6

Politics and Religion

The Renaissance is usually associated with the arts and sciences, but it had more everyday practical consequences for those living at that time. The combination of humanism and classical ideas produced political and religious changes. The result was a reduction in the authority of both government leaders and Catholic priests.

HUMANISM WAS the driving force that emphasized human potential and betterment; this can be seen in the art of Leonardo, Michelangelo and El Greco, the writings of Boccaccio, Dante and Chaucer, and the music of Dunstable, Du Fay and Palestrina. It was not so easy to see upcoming social challenges to despotic leaders who patronized the arts and public projects, or to the clergy who retained active support from many humanists. But changes did occur, however, as the close relationship between politics and religion weakened with individuals assuming more responsibility for their lives, believing they could rise above the class into which they were born. Merchants also took authority from oligarchies by forming committees that put the welfare of their communities first. The Italian city states encouraged their citizens to be active and participate in popular sovereignty, as individualism was an

OPPOSITE: Peter Paul Reubens painted *Glory of St Ignatius of Loyola* in 1616 honouring that founder of the Catholic Jesuit order.

RIGHT: A woodcut by the Swiss artist Jost Amman (1539–91) shows men gathered around a teacher engaging in a heated discussion.

important part of humanism. This was somewhat misleading because the elite continued to retain most of the power. Florence was a republic that advocated a democratic government but was continuously ruled by the party of the Medici, while an equally small minority controlled the republics of Venice and Genoa. The Duchy of Milan was ruled by a succession of dukes who had absolute power. Northern European countries were long ruled by monarchs, but the power slowly began to shift, as seen in the growing independence of Parliament in England.

As political changes spread north in the fifteenth century, they were refined by Christian humanists like Thomas More, who fatally mixed religion and politics in England and Erasmus in Holland. The Catholic Church then suffered a crisis in spiritual and political authority in the sixteenth century, when the Protestant Reformation was led by Martin Luther in Germany and John Calvin in France and Switzerland.

FOREIGN INVASIONS

The Italian city states were attacked during the Renaissance from 1494 to 1559 by France and Spain seeking political control. These Italian Wars began with the invasion in 1494 by France's King Charles VIII (*r.* 1483–98), who took Naples but soon retreated in the face of the alliance of the king of the Romans and future Holy Roman Emperor Maximilian I (1459–1519) and the pope. In 1499, Louis XII of France (*r*. 1498–1515) was victorious over Milan and Genoa, but he was defeated in Naples in 1503 by the Spanish army of Ferdinand V (*r*. 1474–1504) and then driven out of Milan in 1511 by Pope Julius II's Holy League. In 1515, the French army of Francis I (*r*. 1515–47) sought to take Milan and defeated their Swiss allies at the Battle of Marignano (now Melegnano) near Milan. The next year, a peace treaty gave Milan to the French and Spain retained Naples.

In 1521, war between the forces of Holy Roman Emperor Charles V (*r*. 1519–56) and Francis I resulted in the capture of

CITY STATES AT WAR

IN THE LATE FOURTEENTH century, Milan was controlled by the Visconti family, whose cruellest representative was Gian Galeazzo Visconti (1351–1402), the first Duke of Milan. He began several wars that conquered weaker nearby states, including those in coalition with Florence. He overthrew the dynasty in Verona in 1387, forced his rule on Pisa and Siena in 1399, took Perugia the next year and annexed Bologna in June 1402. Three months later, he led a siege of Florence and was close to victory when he died of the plague. By then, the Visconti family controlled most of northern Italy. Florence survived as a strong Renaissance power that took Pisa in 1406.

RIGHT: This illustration shows the 1395 coronation of Visconti as Duke of Milan in the Basilica of Sant'Ambrogio in Milan.

ABOVE: French King
Charles VIII entered
Florence during his
invasion of Italy in
1494, imagined in this
1829 painting by
Giuseppe Bezzuoli.

Francis, who was forced to sign the Treaty of Madrid in 1526,
giving up all claims in Italy. He later reneged on this, but Charles'
soldiers sacked Rome in 1527 and humbled his ally, Pope
Clement VII (r. 1523–34). Francis did give up his claims two
years later in the Treaty of Cambrai. The Italian Wars did not
officially end until 1559, with the Peace of Cateau-Cambresis.

EMPEROR VS. POPE

The Holy Roman Emperor was supposedly the secular equivalent
of the pope. In the fifteenth century, members of the wealthy
Habsburg family were regularly chosen as emperor by the
three archbishops and four German princes, known as electors,
that comprised the empire's electoral college. Allegiance to the
emperor was taken for granted in Germany and Austria, and to a
lesser degree in Italy. His power, however, was in constant conflict
with that of the pope. This became violent in 1527 when troops

OPPOSITE: This miniature
image of the coronation of
Pope Martin V is from the
chronicle of Ulrich von
Richenthal who was there.

of Charles V, who had inherited the Habsburg empire, sacked Rome and humiliated Pope Clement VII, a member of the Medici family, who then had to confirm Charles as emperor in 1530. (Charles had already been proclaimed Holy Roman Emperor by the electors more than a decade earlier, but it was only now, with a papal coronation, that the pope himself officially recognized this.) By 1556, Charles, faced with the Protestant Reformation and continuous hostility from the Vatican, was struggling to hold his empire together. He abdicated his imperial title in favour of his brother, Ferdinand I (*r.* 1556–64), and retired to a monastery.

THE CHURCH HAD ALREADY SURVIVED ONE MAJOR CRISIS WITH THE WESTERN SCHISM THAT LASTED FROM 1378 TO 1417.

Prior to the Reformation, the Church had already survived one major crisis with the Western Schism that lasted from 1378 to 1417, when, at one point, up to three rival popes claimed legitimacy. They denounced one another, weakening the Church and the papacy. This was resolved in 1417 with the election of Martin V (*r.* 1417–31), during the Council of Constance, which lasted from 1414 to 1418. The council also condemned the proto-Protestant teachings of John Wycliffe and Jan Hus, who was burned at the stake during its proceedings. The growth of the Protestant Reformation in the sixteenth century convinced popes to seek changes. Paul III (*r.* 1534–49), who followed Clement VII, reformed the Church and supported the arts and education. His successor Julius III (*r.* 1550–55), patronized Renaissance ideas and called upon the best artisans for the Church, making Michelangelo his head architect and Palestrina, his musical director.

GIROLAMO SAVONAROLA (1452–98)

Born in Ferrara in northern Italy, he entered the Dominican order in Bologna in 1475 and returned to Ferrara in 1478 to teach scripture. He then went to Florence in 1482 as a lecturer in the convent of San Marco, and three years later, in a sermon at San Gimignano in Tuscany, he proposed that the Church had to be reformed. He then preached in several cities until Lorenzo de Medici urged him to return to Florence in 1490, a fatal mistake for the Medici family. Savonarola began preaching about the abuses of the Florentine government, winning popular appeal.

In 1492, he predicted the invasion of Charles VIII, which indeed took place two years later. The Medici were driven

THE SACKING OF ROME

CHARLES V'S ARMY WAS the most powerful armed force in Italy after defeating the French in Pavia in 1525. Two years later, 20,000 of Charles' troops marched on Rome, in protest at being unpaid. Led by the mutinous Charles III, Duke of Bourbon (1490–1527), they included Spanish infantrymen and mercenary German soldiers. On 6 May 1527, they breached the city walls to face some 5000 defenders, including 189 Swiss Guards. The Duke of Bourbon was shot dead, but the attackers nevertheless overwhelmed the city. They looted and destroyed churches and massacred anyone in sight, including children. The civilian death toll numbered 25,000. The Swiss Guard fought to the death on the steps of St Peter's Basilica so that Pope Clement VII could escape via a secret tunnel to the fortress of Castel Sant'Angelo. He surrendered in June, giving Charles a large ransom and much territory.

This engraving shows the death of Charles III during the sack of Rome as he was commanding the imperial soldiers.

out, and Savonarola negotiated with the victorious king to secure a peaceful change of government. He moved into the political vacuum and used his strong sermons to become Florence's ruling force. In his sermons, he predicted the impending deaths of the pope and Lorenzo de Medici. He was obsessed with wickedness and advocated austerity, shunning luxuries and pleasures, replacing carnivals with religious festivals. He particularly denounced the work of Boccaccio and had an impact on Botticelli, who attended his sermons, and Michelangelo, who read them. Both began to add more religious content to their art.

Savonarola then introduced real democracy, sweeping away the old, corrupt politics. This great change created jealousies and led to the establishment of a new party known as the *Arrabbiati* ('the angry ones') to oppose him. The Arrabbiati made alliances with the pope and the Duke of Milan, forming, for example, a Holy League against the French king. When Savonarola refused to join this group, the pope ordered him in 1495 to travel to Bologna or be excommunicated. Savonarola refused, his authority so great that his enemies were left with no choice but to back down.

The tide began to turn after an *Arrabbiati*-led government was formed in Florence. They forced him to stop preaching, provoking a riotous demonstration during which Savonarola and two of his friar-lieutenants were seized, imprisoned and tortured. Later, two papal commissioners arrived from Rome, one of whom declared: 'We shall have a fine bonfire, for I have the sentence of condemnation with me'. They conducted a

ABOVE: Savonarola is shown preaching against luxury and immorality to a crowd in Florence in this engraving published about 1880.

brief trial, found the three men guilty and sentenced them to be hanged and burned. On 24 May 1498, Savonarola and his two colleagues were taken to Florence's Piazza della Signoria where the scaffold and crowds awaited. They were hanged from a beam above fires that consumed their dead bodies. Savonarola was the last to be executed, and when a priest asked how he felt about his martyrdom, he replied, 'The Lord has suffered as much for me'.

THOMAS MORE (1478–1535)

He was born in London to a lawyer and judge and attended St Anthony's School in London. In 1490, he became a page to the Archbishop of Canterbury, the humanist John Morton (c. 1420–1500). From 1492 to 94, More studied Latin and formal logic at Oxford University and then trained in London as a lawyer. He began his practice in 1502 but then spent time between 1503 and 1504 in a Carthusian monastery. He was elected to Parliament in 1504 and became Privy Counselor in 1514. Henry VIII (r. 1509–47) admired his integrity and piety, knighting him in 1521.

More's *Utopia* (Greek for 'nowhere') was written with humanists in mind and published in 1516 as a satire to help reform English politics and society. It describes a pagan city

OPPOSITE: Sir Thomas More was painted on an oak panel by the German artist Hans Holbein, who received the commission in 1527.

LEFT: The first edition of Thomas More's *Utopia* in 1516 contained a woodcut illustration of the ideal island (*Utopiae Insulae*).

state governed by reason, featuring religious tolerance and honest politicians, espousing a humanist philosophy that politicians should win support for their policies by using an indirect approach. More became Henry VIII's Lord Chancellor in 1529. But the two men fell out when More opposed the king's divorce from Katherine of Aragon, refusing to sign a letter to the pope requesting an annulment. Their relationship worsened in 1534 when More refused to take the Oath of Supremacy that recognized Henry as head of the Church of England. Accused of treason, More was convicted in 15 minutes and was sentenced to be hung, drawn and quartered, but Henry commuted this to beheading. More spent 15 months in the Tower of London and was executed for treason in 1535. On the scaffold, he proclaimed he was dying 'in the faith and for the faith of the Catholic Church, the king's good servant and God's first'. The Catholic Church canonized him in 1935.

BELOW: This 1523 portrait of Erasmus was by Hans Holbein the Younger. Erasmus was so pleased with the portrait he sent copies around Europe.

ERASMUS (1466–1536)
He was born as Desiderius Erasmus in Rotterdam, Holland, the illegitimate son of a priest and studied at the small town of Deventer where the headmaster and his teacher were humanists. His parents died about 1483 from the plague, and in 1485 his guardian consigned him to an Augustinian monastery in Steyn. He spent seven years there and was ordained as a Catholic priest in 1492, although he never became an active one. Erasmus

then served as secretary to the bishop of Chambrey, who in 1495 sent him to Paris to study theology and classical literature; while there, he again came into contact with humanists.

In Paris, Erasmus became a noted lecturer. One of his students was so impressed with Erasmus that he established a pension allowing him to travel in several countries as a lecturer, meeting some of Europe's greatest scholars. He went to England in 1499 and met Thomas More, staying in his home, and John Colet (1467–1519), the humanist and theologian he had known in Paris. Both men became lifelong friends and were great influences on Erasmus.

He began teaching at Cambridge in the early 1500s, lecturing in theology. In Thomas More's house, he wrote *Moriae Encomium* (*In Praise of Folly*), a satire on the sins and abuses in society and the Church, with a special condemnation of war, which he compared to the plague. In 1514, Erasmus wrote *Familiarium Colloquiorum Formulae* (*Forms of Familiar Conversation*), more commonly called *Colloquies,* in which he attacked greedy clergymen, fake miracles and meaningless rituals. It was popular with readers, but authorities in France ordered that the book be burned, while Charles V of Spain said those reading it should be executed. In 1516, Erasmus translated the New Testament into Greek, a dangerous challenge to the Church. After Martin Luther published his *95 Theses* in 1517, Erasmus supported Protestant goals but disliked the radical methods of Luther. Although Erasmus was loyal to the Catholic Church, he believed the relationship to God should be a personal one. When he died, he did not ask to receive last rites.

ABOVE: An edition of Colloquies with a hand-coloured engraving was published in Basel in 1537, a year after Erasmus' death.

MACHIAVELLI (1469–1527)

Niccolò Machiavelli was born in Florence to an aristocratic family, and little is known about his early life. In 1498, he became chancellor and secretary of the Florentine Republic

BELOW: A marble statue of Machiavelli (misspelt 'Macchiavelli') stands outside the Uffizi Gallery in Florence. It was created by Lorenzo Bartolini.

while the ruling Medici family was in exile and he went on 23 diplomatic missions, including four to the French king. In one report from 1503, he describes the political murders committed by Cesare Borgia, the Duke Valentinois. Machiavelli stayed at Borgia's court for several months in 1502 and later used him as the inspiration for his book, *The Prince*. Also that year, he married Marrietta Corsini and they had four sons and two daughters.

In 1512, after serving Florence for 14 years, Machiavelli was incorrectly arrested, imprisoned and tortured as a conspirator against the Medici who had been reinstated that year. The following year, he wrote the work for which is best known, *The Prince*. Machiavelli's reputation as an advocate of ruthless *realpolitik* was fixed by the book's Chapter 17, 'On Cruelty Or Clemency, and Whether It Is Better To Be Loved Or Feared', in which he said the innate badness of men means that the prince should instil fear instead of love in his subjects. This concept has been both criticized and praised ever since – more so the former than the latter, admittedly, although the second president of the United States, John Adams, was one prominent and powerful subscriber to the idea that mankind responds better to the stick than the carrot. A more inspiring theme of the work is its humanistic contention that man should be free to determine his own destiny instead of being controlled by the church or fate.

Machiavelli's many other writings included poetry, plays and carnival songs. In 1521, he published *Arte della Guerra* (*The Art of War*) a work about military tactics that emphasized the important link between the military and civilian worlds, citing the stability the civilian militia gave to the Roman Republic. In 1526, Pope Clement VII commissioned him to inspect Florence's fortifications and he was sent on two diplomatic missions by the Papal Commissary of War in Lombardy.

NICCOLÒ MACCHIAVELLI

Machiavelli died the following year and, despite his constant criticism of the Catholic Church, he received the last rites.

CESARE BORGIA(1475–1507)

He was born in Rome, the son of a cardinal, Rodrigo Borgia (1431–1503), and from 1489 studied law at the University of Perugia and then received a law degree from the University of Pisa. When his father became Pope Alexander VI in 1492, Cesare was made archbishop of Valencia and the next year became a cardinal. In 1497, his brother Giovanni, Duke of Gandia, was murdered and many suspected Cesare of the deed in order to gain his father's full attention.

Cesare Borgia went to Naples in 1497 as the pope's representative and crowned Frederick of Aragon as king. The following year, he successfully petitioned the pope for permission to renounce the priesthood. In 1499, with the military help of France's King Louis XII, he achieved victories in Romagna in northern Italy and returned to receive many honours from his father, the pope.

ABOVE: This 1518 portrait of Borgia by the Italian painter Giovanni di Lutero is titled *Portrait d'homme* (Portrait of a Man).

In 1500, Borgia was suspected of arranging the murder of his brother-in-law Alfonso, Duke of Bisceglie (1481–1500), who was attacked on the steps of St Peter's and critically wounded. Although he survived, Alfonso was murdered a month later as he lay recovering from the initial assault.

In October 1500, Cesare Borgia returned to Romagna to take more cities. The people of Faenza held out due to their devotion to 18-year-old Astorre Manfredi, their handsome lord. He surrendered in 1501 after Borgia's promise of clemency. Instead, Borgia sent him to Rome where he was executed. By now, Borgia's reputation for cruelty was terrorizing Italy. A conspiracy of his former princes and captains led to some military defeats, but it finally dissipated when the French king promised to send help to Borgia.

Back in Rome in 1503, Cesare Borgia and his father both came down with fever. His father died that year and Borgia tried in vain to block the election of an enemy, Giuliano della Rovere, who became Pope Julius II (r. 1503–30). He demanded that Borgia's territories be returned to the Church and had him arrested, and was only released in order to arrange the surrender of his castles. In Naples, under Spanish control, he was arrested again and sent to Spain where he was imprisoned for two years. He escaped in 1506, finding refuge with his brother-in-law, King John III of Navarre (r. 1484–1516), and was killed on 11 March 1507 helping besiege the castle of Viana held by a rebellious count. Cesare Borgia was at first buried beneath the altar of Viana's Church of Santa Maria but was later re-interred in unconsecrated ground after, the story goes, the Bishop of Calahorra while visiting the church was shocked and outraged to discover such a sinner laying at rest there. Finally, on 11 March 2007, Cesare Borgia's remains were reburied in the church 500 years after his death.

WYCLIFFE'S FOLLOWERS, GENERALLY KNOWN AS LOLLARDS, CONTINUED HIS BELIEFS IN THE FACE OF SEVERE REPRISALS.

THE PROTESTANT REFORMATION

Church reforms advocated in the late 1300s by John Wycliffe in England anticipated the Protestant Reformation to come. He equated the pope with the anti-Christ, believed the Bible was the ultimate religious authority, wanted to abolish the selling of indulgences to avoid punishments for sin and disbelieved in transubstantiation (that the bread and wine used at communion became Christ's actual body and blood). Wycliffe's followers, generally known as Lollards, continued his beliefs in the face of severe reprisals. The Czech priest Jan Hus was greatly influenced by Wycliffe and was burned at the stake in 1415 for his Wycliffite heresy.

One act by one man, an Augustinian monk, began the end of Roman Catholicism's monopoly of Christianity and led to religious persecution and wars that lasted for centuries. Martin Luther began the protest in 1517 by supposedly nailing his *95*

OPPOSITE: This sixteenth-century print in Germany was a Lutheran satirical criticism of the sale of indulgencies by the papacy.

Theses to a chapel door in Wittenberg, Germany. This was done as an act of complaint against the abuses of the Catholic Church, not with the intention of forming a separate religion. However, by the mid-sixteenth century, those opposing Catholicism began to unite in what would become the Protestant faith. Luther's reforms eventually led to the establishment of the Lutheran

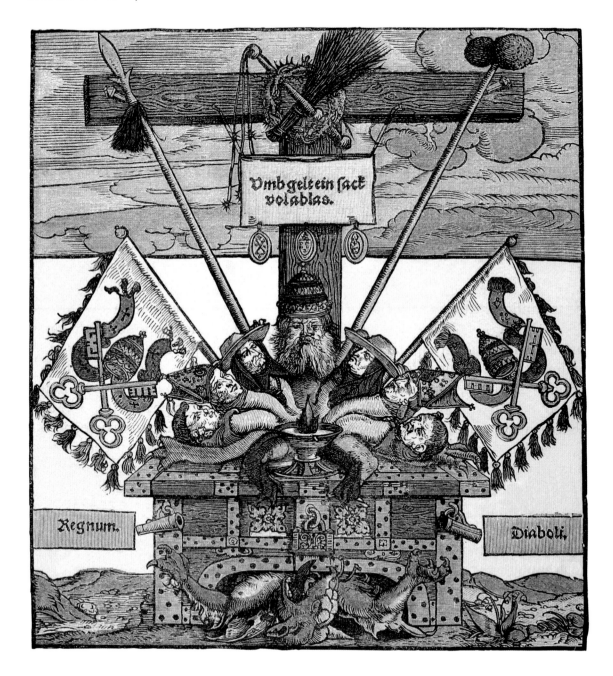

Church, and the ideas of John Calvin in France became the founding principles of the Presbyterian Church.

The result was most clearly seen in England, where Henry VIII broke with the Vatican when it refused to grant him a divorce from Catherine of Aragon (1485–1536). Henry then established the Church of England and declared himself its head. He abolished Catholic monasteries and persecuted those who would not recognize his new role as a religious leader, even beheading his Lord Chancellor, Thomas More. This was only the beginning of Catholic-Protestant conflicts that included Henry's daughter, as Queen Mary I (*r.* 1553–58), attempting to reestablish Catholicism by force, for example by burning Protestants at the stake.

The Counter-Reformation by the Catholic Church began under Paul III to defend against the Protestant Reformation and make changes within the Church to defer the strongest criticisms against it. He received strong support from priests such as Spain's Ignatius of Loyola and the formation of new Catholic orders, such as the Jesuits, Ursulines and Capuchins. Other measures included the discipline of the corrupt clergy, more seminaries to better prepare future priests, increased missionary work around the world, attacks on the doctrines of Protestants and an index of forbidden books to stop the spread of Protestant writings.

JOHN WYCLIFFE (1330–84)

Born in Yorkshire, Wycliffe (also spelt Wycliff) studied at Oxford around 1350 and was ordained a priest the following year. He was elected master of Oxford's Balliol College in 1361. The government sent him to Bruges, Belgium, in 1374 to negotiate clerical

BELOW: As Wycliffe was dying, hostile clerics gathered at his deathbed hoping he would recant, but he was unable to speak.

HENRY VIII, AS AUTHOR

BEFORE HE BROKE WITH the Catholic Church in Rome, Henry VIII was one of its strongest supporters. While a young king, he was offended by Luther's *95 Theses*, responding with a book of 30,000 words written in Latin, *Assertio Septem Sacramentorum Adversus Martinum Lutherum* (*Defence of the Seven Sacraments Against Martin Luther*), the first book ever written by an English monarch. It was so popular, 20 editions were published. Scholars generally believe Henry wrote most of the text, although some feel he had ample help, most probably from Thomas More. The book criticizes Luther for his 'impertinent calumnies' and defends papal authority and the indissolubility of marriage. After its publication in 1521, Pope Leo X (*r.* 1513–21) named Henry 'Defender of the Faith'. When Henry broke with Rome in 1534, becoming head of the Church of England, Pope Paul III rescinded the title, but in 1544 Parliament restored it to Henry and all future British monarchs.

taxes with a papal deputation, and that year he became rector of Lutterworth in Leicestershire.

Wycliffe disagreed with the Catholic Church on several matters, disbelieving in transubstantiation and criticizing the Church's landed wealth and the corruption of the clergy, such as through the selling of indulgences. He also believed the Church wanted to enforce its authority by keeping the Bible in Latin, a language that the great majority of Catholics could not understand. Pope Gregory XI (*r.* 1370–78) issued five papal bulls against him. He was in constant danger of being arrested for heresy, but powerful friends and lucky fate came to his rescue. From 1376 to 1378, he was a clerical advisor to John of Gaunt (1340–99), the Duke of Lancaster and the effective ruler of England during the early reign of the young Richard II (*r.* 1377–99). When Wycliffe was called to the King's Council in 1376 to be questioned about his beliefs, a riot broke out and the council was abandoned. After he made a systematic attack on the Church, he was called that year for another investigation in London, but this was broken up by a representative of the king's mother. In 1380,

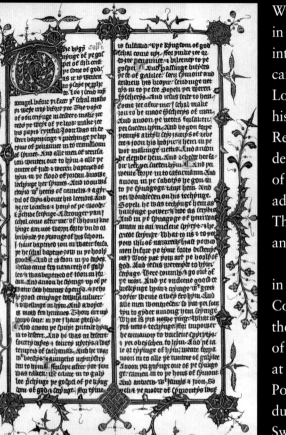

ABOVE: Shown is a page of St Mark's gospel from the first of two English versions of the Bible instigated by Wycliffe.

Wycliffe began to instigate what resulted in two translations of the complete Bible into English. His worst condemnation came in 1382, by the Blackfriars Council in London, regarding the possible influence of his views on the previous year's Peasants' Revolt, an uprising that resulted in the death of the Archbishop of Canterbury. All of Wycliffe's writings were banned and, to add to his misfortunes, he suffered a stroke. This was followed, two years later, by another stroke that proved fatal.

Wycliffe was condemned as a heretic in 1415 by the ecclesiastical Council of Constance in Germany. That same year, the council convicted Jan Hus, a follower of Wycliffe, of heresy, and he was burned at the stake. In 1428, on the orders of Pope Martin V, Wycliffe's bones were dug up, burned and scattered in the river Swift that flows through Lutterworth. Nevertheless, Wycliffe has been called 'the morning star of the Reformation', and his controversial views were retained and spread by his followers known as the Lollards.

JAN HUS (1369–1415)

Born in Bohemia (now part of the Czech Republic) of poor parents, Hus (also spelt Huss) entered the University of Prague in 1390 and received a master's degree in 1396. He became a professor of theology there and in 1400 was ordained a priest. In 1409 he was named rector of the university. He became involved with the reform movement of the Czech Jan Milíč (1325–74) who was influenced by John Wycliffe.

Hus used sermons in Czech, preaching in the Bethlehem Chapel in Prague that became a rallying point for Church reform. He denounced abuses by the clergy, calling for them to hold spiritual, not earthly, powers, and for consecrated bread to be distributed to Christians during communion. He also advocated a return to poverty and in 1412 published *Questio de Indulentis* (*Investigation of Indulgences*) against the selling of indulgences.

That year, Hus was excommunicated by his archbishop for insubordination. In 1414, he was summoned to the Council of Constance. Germany's King Sigismund falsely guaranteed his safety on the journey both ways, even if found guilty, he said. The council ordered him to recant his views on the Church, but Hus refused. He stated that the papacy was not created by God but by the Church to keep its affairs in order. He was found guilty of heresy and burned at the stake on 6 July 1415. A paper crown decorated with images of devils had been put on his head, and at the stake, he was given another chance to recant to save his life, but he again refused.

The militant followers of Hus were called Hussites. They conducted a rebellion from 1419 to 1436 and won victories over

BELOW: *Master Jan Hus Preaching at the Bethlehem Chapel* was painted in 1916 by the Czech artist Alfons Mucha.

5

5

troops sent by the pope and the king of Bohemia. The Hussites eventually controlled all of Bohemia, and the Church negotiated a compromise with its moderate members who then helped to defeat Hussite extremists. Other followers of Hus became known as Moravians, and their Moravian Church still exists.

MARTIN LUTHER (1483–1546)

He was born in Eisleben, Saxony (now Germany), the son of a copper miner. In 1501, he began studying at the University of Erfurt and received his master's degree in 1505. However, he chose to join a monastic order and was ordained an Augustinian friar in 1507. He continued studies at the University of Erfurt and also at the University of Wittenberg where he taught and became a doctor of Theology in 1512.

Luther represented several Augustinian monasteries on a visit to Rome in 1510 and was shocked by the level of church corruption that was apparent. He was particularly appalled by the selling of letters of indulgences whereby people could buy a remission of their sins. On 31 October 1517, Luther defied the most powerful institution of his day by publishing his *95 Theses* that he nailed to the chapel door at the University of Wittenberg. Other accounts say he posted it to Archbishop Albert of Mainz. This series of questions and propositions for debate criticized papal abuses, especially the selling of indulgences. Luther called them 'nets with which one fishes for the wealth of people'. He specifically deplored the Church's decision to raise funds from indulgences to renovate St Peter's Basilica in Rome, asking: 'Why does not the pope, whose wealth today is greater than the

BELOW: After hearing Luther lecture, one impressed student said he combined a sharpness of enunciation with a softness of tone.

wealth of the richest Crassus, build the basilica of St Peter with his own money rather than with the money of poor believers?' (Pope Pius V abolished the sale of indulgences in 1567.)

The *95 Theses* also carried the messages that the Bible was the source of religious authority, not the Church, and that only individual faith and divine grace led to salvation, an assertion which opposed the church's view that 'good deeds' were necessary for salvation. (The Church resisted this doctrine until the 1960s.)

These ideas were the beginning of the Protestant Reformation. In 1518, Luther was called to an Imperial Diet in Augsburg. After a three-day debate with Cardinal Thomas Cajetan (1469–1534), Luther refused to recant. He followed this between 1519 and 1520 with several pamphlets, including *On Christian Liberty* and *On the Freedom of a Christian Man*. All of these ideas were printed and circulated through Europe, giving his protests an immense influence. Pope Leo X excommunicated him on 3 January 1521 and on 17 April Luther was ordered to appear before the Diet of Worms assembly in Germany, where he again refused to recant. Emperor Charles V declared him a heretic and outlaw and ordered his books to be burned. Luther hid for nearly a year in Wartburg Castle near Eisenach and in 1522 returned to Wittenberg. In 1525, Luther,

A SPECIAL MARRIAGE

MARTIN LUTHER's wife was the nun Katharina von Bora (1499–1552). She became dissatisfied with life in her Nimbschen convent and asked Luther to help her, and several other nuns to escape, an offence punishable by death. He agreed, and on 4 April 1523 arranged for them to escape by hiding in a consignment of empty herring barrels. When Luther expressed his intention to marry Katherina, friends warned it would harm the revolution he had started, but he said it would 'rile the pope, cause the angels to laugh and the devils to weep'. They wed on 13 June 1525. Luther was 41 and Katherina 26. The couple had six children and settled in the Black Cloister monastery in Wittenberg, where Luther gave Katherina complete control of the household and a farm they owned. As he noted: 'There is no more lovely, friendly and charming relationship, communion or company than a good marriage'.

Katharina von Bora's portrait at the age of 27 was painted in 1526 by Lucas Cranach the Elder.

who was opposed to clerical celibacy, married a former nun, Katharina von Bora, and they had six children.

Luther lost support between 1524 and 1526 when he failed to support the Peasants' War in Germany, a rebellion whose leaders based their revolt on his ideas. He expressed sympathy for their cause but condemned their actions and demands, even agreeing that the authorities were correct to suppress the uprising.

In 1534, Luther published his translation of the Bible in German, a long labour that began during his stay in Wartburg

Castle. It followed his belief that Germans should be able to read the book in their own language. His last writings were strident pieces against the Jews, the papacy (calling the pope 'the Anti-Christ') and the Anabaptists radical reformers.

Luther's ideas were carried on by the doctrine of Lutheranism that has led to Lutheran churches mostly in Europe and North America with more than 72 million members, making Lutherans the second largest Protestant denomination after Baptists.

JOHN CALVIN (1509–64)

He was born Jean Calvin(or Cauvin) in Noyon, France, the son of a lay assistant to the local bishop. His father wanted him to prepare for the priesthood, and in 1523 sent him at the age of 14 to the University of Paris where he came into contact with humanistic learning. He earned his master's degree at 18, but his father decided his son should change to law, so young Calvin moved on to Orleans, receiving his doctorate in law there by 1532. That year, he also published his first book, a commentary on Seneca's *De Clementia* (*On Mercy*).

After Calvin collaborated on a strong speech on religious principles to be given by the university's rector, his rooms in Paris were searched and his writings confiscated by authorities searching for heretical material. He fled back to Noyon and then to Basel, Switzerland, where in 1536 he completed his *Institutes of the Christian Religion*. It gained a wide readership, and Calvin revised it in 1539. He then published Latin editions in 1543, 1550 and 1559, as well as French language ones in 1545 and 1560.

Calvin began preaching almost daily in the Catholic town of Geneva, Switzerland, but the city council rejected his rigid religious views and he was expelled in 1538. He settled in Protestant Strasbourg for three years with a congregation and began writing commentaries

BELOW: Although Calvin advocated submission to those having legitimate authority, he called for resistance to leaders opposing the spread of Protestantism.

RIGHT: Calvin is shown with council officials who joined him in founding the seminary in 1559 which became the College of Geneva.

on nearly every book of the Bible. He took part in international religious conferences and became a renowned Protestant leader. Geneva's council called him back in 1541, and he was able to convince them to ratify his *Ecclesiastical Ordinances of the Church of Geneva* that included policies of a reformed church.

Calvin also welcomed the religious refugees that poured into Geneva from countries intolerant of Protestantism, mostly from France but also other European nations and England. He established an academy that taught humanism to students who would be future priests and government leaders. By then, Calvin had become the most influential living leader of the Protestant Reformation. He remained in Geneva for the remainder of his life and was buried in an unmarked grave, following his wish to avoid any possible worship by his followers. His theology developed into Calvinism and spread throughout Europe, Britain (especially as the Church of Scotland) and North America.

OPPOSITE: German artist Gerlach Flicke painted this portrait of Cranmer in 1545 at the height of his religious influence under Henry VIII.

THOMAS CRANMER (1489–1556)

He was born in Nottinghamshire, the son of gentry, and in 1510 received a fellowship to Jesus College, Cambridge. This was withdrawn after Cranmer married a tavern keeper's daughter who died in childbirth. His college then readmitted him, and

he took holy orders in 1523. The plague forced him to move to Essex, where he encountered Henry VIII who was visiting nearby. Henry convinced Cranmer of his need to divorce Catherine of Aragon, and they agreed that Cranmer would be a good advocate for that cause. He argued the case to Rome in 1530 and two years later became an ambassador to the Holy Roman Emperor Charles V. Cranmer was then dispatched to Germany to learn about Lutheranism and there met and married the niece of a Lutheran reformer.

Cranmer was named Archbishop of Canterbury in 1533. After this was approved by the pope (who did not know of Cranmer's marriage), Cranmer declared Henry's marriage void and four months later married him to Anne Boleyn (1507–1536). He encouraged the translation of the Bible into English and in 1545 wrote a litany still used in the church. During the reign of

BELOW: This woodcut shows the martyrdom of Cranmer in Oxford's town ditch as he thrusts his hand into the flames.

L, Receiue my spirit.

Frier John.

Edward VI (*r.* 1547–53), he made changes in the church's doctrines. He also helped complete the *Book of Common Prayer* in 1549.

When Edward VI died, Cranmer supported the succession of Lady Jane Grey (1537–54), but she only reigned for nine days and Mary I, a Roman Catholic, took the throne. She tried Cranmer for treason, and although forced to publicly proclaim his error in believing in Protestantism he was still condemned to be burned at the stake. This took place in Oxford on 21 March 1556. Famously, Cranmer put the hand that had signed his recantation into the fire first.

IGNATIUS OF LOYOLA (1491–1556)

Born Inigo de Loyola, he was the thirteenth child of Basque noble parents. In 1501, he became a page in Arevalo at the court of Juan Velazquez de Cuellar (*c.* 1460–1517), the treasurer general of King Ferdinand. He joined the military in 1517 and fought the French at Pamplona until suffering a leg wound on 20 May 1521. While recovering, he read devotional works that led to his conversion. In 1522, he retired to do penance, first in a monastery in Montserrat and then Manresa, followed by a pilgrimage to Jerusalem.

Inigo entered the University of Paris in 1528 to study theology and philosophy, receiving a master of arts degree in 1534. While there, he Latinized his name to Ignatius and became part of a small group of six who took vows of poverty and chastity on 15 August 1534 to work for the glory of God and travel to Jerusalem. Also among the six was Francis Xavier who would become a missionary to Asia. Ignatius and some others in the group were ordained on 24 June 1537 in Venice.

When the Jerusalem trip proved impossible, Ignatius in 1538 asked Pope Paul III for permission to form a new order that the group had already named *Compania de Jesus* ('Society of Jesus').

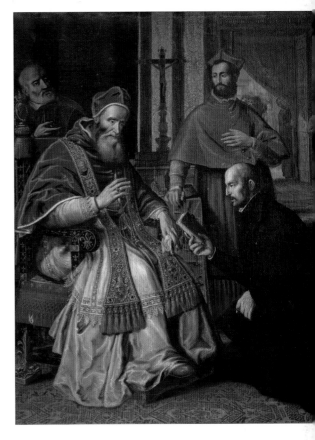

ABOVE: **Pope Paul III was impressed by Ignatius' appeal in 1538 to establish a new order that became the Jesuits.**

This was approved by papal bull in 1540, and Ignatius was named its superior general, a post he held in Rome for the rest of his life. The Jesuits, as the group came to be known, tended to the poor, built hospitals and sent missionaries around the world. Most of all, they established colleges throughout Europe, believing education would strengthen the Catholic renewal. After instructions from Ignatius, Peter Canisius (1521–97), later a saint, supervised the opening of 37 colleges in Italy and Spain. In the same year that the Jesuit order was founded, Ignatius also published *Spiritual Exercises*, a collection of prayers, meditations and contemplations designed to help readers discover God's purpose in their lives. His other main writing, *Constitutions*, printed in 1550, dealt with the spiritual development of a Jesuit, advocating absolute loyalty to the Church and the commands of the pope.

Also in 1550, Ignatius began to believe that the main work of the Jesuits should be opposing the Protestant Reformation. Among his Counter-Reformation strategies were luring back Catholics who had become Protestants, encouraging baptisms for those who had not been baptized, reviving the faith of Catholics and training Jesuit members for missionary work and social service.

By the time of his death in 1556, Ignatius had seen the Jesuits grow to more than 1000 members. The Roman Catholic Church made him a saint in 1622.

BELOW: **This illustration is from Ignatius'** *Examen Conscientiae* **(***Examination of Conscience***) in a 1689 publication of** *Exercitia Spiritualia* **(***Spirtual Exercises***).**

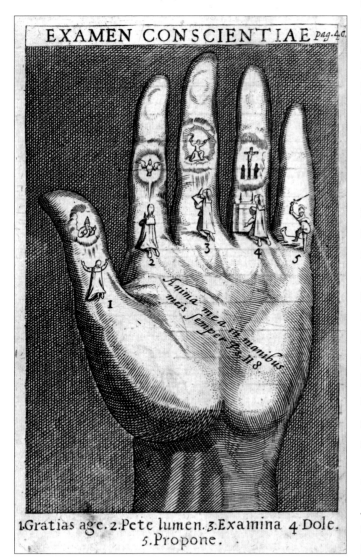

EXAMEN CONSCIENTIAE pag. 40.

1.Gratias age. 2.Pete lumen. 3.Examina 4 Dole. 5.Propone.

JOHN KNOX (*c.*1514–1572)

Little is known about Knox's early life other than his birthplace
near Haddington in southeastern Scotland. He apparently studied
for the priesthood at the University of St Andrews without taking
his master's degree. He was a priest by 1540 and a notary three
years later. In 1545, he was tutoring in East Lothian where he
became acquainted with George Wishart,
a Scottish Reformation leader who was
preaching in the area. Knox was converted
to his Protestant beliefs, but in 1546 Wishart
was burned at the stake for heresy. Knox
took his pupils from place to place to avoid
persecution, finally spending three months
with other Protestants in St Andrews castle. While there, others
persuaded him to begin preaching for the Reformation.

BY THE TIME OF HIS DEATH IN
1556, IGNATIUS HAD SEEN THE
JESUITS GROW TO MORE THAN
1000 MEMBERS.

In 1447, French soldiers arrived to support the governor
of Scotland and captured the castle, taking Knox and others
as slaves. They were released 19 months later through an
English appeal. Knox received strong support from Edward VI's
Protestant government who retained him as an advocate for the
Reformation, sending him to preach around the country. This
ended in 1553 when Mary Tutor, a Roman Catholic, ascended
to the throne. Knox fled to Europe and became minister to
Protestant English refugees in Frankfurt am Main, Germany, and
Geneva, Switzerland. Between 1555 and 1556, he visited Scotland
where he urged Protestants to resist Roman Catholic rulers.

After returning to Geneva, he formulated and wrote his treatise
on predestination and another one on the 'monstrous' rule of
women in government. While in Geneva, Queen Mary died, to
be succeeded by the Protestant Elizabeth I (*r.* 1558–1603). This
allowed Knox to return to Edinburgh in 1559 to preach and
help the weakening Protestant cause (it should be remembered
that Scotland, at that time, was politically and constitutionally
separate from England and was ruled by its own monarch, the
Catholic Mary I, more commonly known to history as Mary,
Queen of Scots. Mary was just 17 at this time, and had been
living in France since her early childhood while regents governed

OPPOSITE: This portrait of Elizabeth I by an unknown English artist was painted about 1588 to celebrate the defeat of the Spanish Armada.

Scotland in her stead). That same year Knox also began work on his five-volume book, *The History of the Reformation in Scotland*, completed in 1566.

French intervention in Scotland caused Elizabeth to unite with Protestants there and their combined force caused the French to withdraw. In 1560, Knox presented his *First Book of Discipline* to the Scottish Parliament. It outlined his ideas on the organization of the reformed church, proposals that would become part of the Presbyterian Church. They included elections by the people of ministers and elders who would govern the congregations.

Knox died in 1572, having suffered a stroke two years earlier from which he never fully recovered. In the years before his death, Knox had clashed several times with Mary I (*r.* 1542–67), who had finally returned to Scotland from her French exile in 1561. Her return only exacerbated widening tensions between Catholics and Protestants in the country, of which her disagreements with the uncompromising and unbending Knox were the most prominent example.

A TRAGIC CHILDHOOD

SHE WOULD BECOME ONE of England's most powerful and beloved monarchs, an amazing feat considering Elizabeth's youth. Born in 1533, before she was three, her father Henry VIII had her mother Anne Boleyn beheaded. He then declared Elizabeth illegitimate and not eligible to succeed to the throne. Her title was reduced from princess to lady. Her father died when she was 13, and Elizabeth lived with her stepmother Catherine Parr until 1548 when Catherine's concerns over her husband Thomas Seymour's relationship with the teenage Elizabeth caused her to be sent away. After Catherine died later that same year, Seymour was executed, after being accused of planning to marry Elizabeth and kidnap Edward VI, her 10-year-old half-brother who had become king. Edward died in 1553 and Elizabeth's older sister, Mary, became queen. She returned the country to Catholicism, instigated many executions and imprisoned Elizabeth in the Tower of London, then later under house arrest. After Mary's death in 1558, Elizabeth became queen at 25.

CHAPTER 7

Legacy

The Renaissance was a rebirth of the classic wisdom of ancient Greeks and Romans. It sought to eliminate the superstitions and stagnation of the Middle Ages. It would replace the helplessness of individuals before authority with their own ideas and initiatives. It would change the world in every possible way one could imagine.

IN SHORT, people found new ways of doing things better in the Renaissance. Its humanistic outlook demonstrated what an individual could achieve. For the first time it brought together the arts, sciences and philosophy, then for the first time passed the information to distant locations. This revitalized Europe and eventually led to the industrial revolution, making Europe the dominant global power for centuries. Even those who could not read were affected by the dramatic changes around them, including more democratic systems of government. One advance quickly led to another, and this sowed the seeds for the modern world.

Changes and advances made in the Renaissance still exist. The realism and perspectives of today's portraits and other art can be traced back to the innovations of Giotto, Brunelleschi, Dürer and other Renaissance artists. Today's knowledge of anatomy

OPPOSITE: Michelangelo's paintings on the Sistine Chapel's ceiling are world famous. The ceiling was originally painted blue and covered with golden stars.

and surgery is the end result of dissections carried out by artists like Leonardo, Michelangelo and Rubens. Leonardo was also the first to envision the helicopter, submarine and parachute. Today's double-entry bookkeeping was handed down by Luca Pacioli. Astronomers like Copernicus and Galileo initiated our understanding of earth's place in the solar system. Libraries now filled with books owe much to Gutenberg's first printing press with movable type, and books written in their countries' own languages began with Dante, Boccaccio, Cervantes and Chaucer. Music became more dramatic and led to the creation of opera. Many new countries were established because of the bold voyages of such explorers as Columbus, Magellan and Drake, with Vespucci giving his name to America. Churches like the Lutheran, Presbyterian, Church of England and Episcopal denominations are impressive outgrowths of the Protestant Reformation virtually begun by one man, Martin Luther.

ABOVE: The Gutenberg Museum in Mainz, Germany has reconstructed his workshop and has old printing presses and two original Gutenberg Bibles.

THE ARTS

The Renaissance elevated the professional and social positions of artists. They had been considered craftsmen, but the patronage of powerful leaders like the Medici family won them respect and fame. Their works glorified both God and man. Art became more available to the general public as large murals were commissioned to decorate council halls and display civic accomplishments.

The revival of classical sculpture and architecture led to awesome buildings, monuments and statues, highly visible symbols of a city state's wealth and power. They also led to new public esteem for the architects and sculptors whose names became well known through Italy and beyond.

EDOUARD MANET (1832–83)

Manet was greatly influenced by Renaissance painters, especially Titian. Born in Paris, he was the son of a high-ranking judge. In 1850, he began six years of training in the Paris studio of Thomas Couture (1815–79), who loved Venetian painting. Also that year, Manet became a copyist in the Louvre. In 1853, he travelled to Venice and in 1857 to Florence where he copied Titian's *Venus of Urbino* and later incorporated some of its features, including the rich colours, into his celebrated but controversial nude *Olympia* (1863). That year, he also displayed his Impressionist masterpiece featuring another nude,

LEFT: Manet was one of the most controversial artists of his day and suffered years of criticism before gaining fame.

BELOW: Manet's *Le Déjeuner sur l'herbe* (*The Luncheon on the Grass*) was too shocking to be accepted by the Paris Salon.

RIGHT: Titian's *Le Concert Champetre* (*Pastoral Concert*) painted about 1509 was the inspiration for Monet's *The Luncheon on the Grass*.

Le Déjeuner sur l'herbe (*The Luncheon on the Grass*) an updated version of Titian's *Pastoral Concert*. It was one of his works rejected by the Paris Salon but accepted by the *Salon des Refusés*, an exhibit of rejected paintings.

Manet also drew on other Renaissance artists for inspiration. His *Jesus Mocked by the Soldiers* (1865) was influenced by two works, *Christ Crowned with Thorns* by Titian and *The Dead Christ Supported by an Angel* by Antonello da Messina (*c.* 1430 –79), a Sicilian painter active in Venice. Manet's *The Balcony* (1868–69) owes much to *Two Venetian Ladies* by the Venetian painter Vittore Carpaccio (1465–1520).

Manet again visited Venice in 1874. In 1881 he was made a Chevalier of the Legion of Honour.

THE NUDE CONTINUES

Manet's nudes shocked the public because of the languid reclining pose in *Olympia* and the casual pose of a nude woman surrounded by men wearing suits in *Le Déjeuner sur l'herbe*. There was little controversy, however, when Renaissance artists revived the classic nude that had virtually been banished during

WHEN MANET MET MONET

THEIR RELATIONSHIP BEGAN ON a wrong note, when Manet complained, 'Who is this Monet whose name sounds just like mine and who is taking advantage of my notoriety?' Things became worse in 1865, in the Paris Salon, when people mistakenly congratulated Manet on seascape paintings done by Monet, who was nine years younger. 'Who is this rascal who pastiches my painting so basely?' Manet grumbled. The two soon met there, however, and swapped compliments about each other's works. They became friends, and Manet even painted Monet and his family in 1874. The work shows Monet's influence on Manet to become more impressionistic, though the older painter refused to take part in Impressionist exhibitions. As he painted the Monet family, the artist Auguste Renoir (1841–1919) joined them and also began to paint them, irritating Manet. 'He has no talent, that boy,' Manet told Monet. 'Since he's your friend, you should tell him to give up painting.'

Manet produced *Monet Painting on his Studio Boat* in 1874 when Monet was living at Argenteuil near Paris.

ABOVE: Manet's *Olympia* was considered scandalous because its realism failed to elevate the figure to the ideal of classic nudity.

OPPOSITE: Frederic Leighton's *An Athlete Wrestling with a Python* was an example of Britain's 'New Sculpture' movement that he pioneered.

the Middle Ages. Leonardo used the male nude for his famous sketch, *Vitruvian Man* (*c.* 1490) and Antonio Pollaiuolo used 10 for his engraving *Battle of the Nudes* (*c.* 1470–95). Nudes even became acceptable for religious paintings, such as Masaccio's depiction of Adam and Eve in *The Expulsion* (1425–28) and Dürer's *Adam and Eve* (1504). The nude became monumental with heroic statues. The Medici family commissioned Donatello's bronze *David* (*c.* 1440s), the first large free-standing male nude statue since classical times. Michelangelo's massive marble *David* (1502–04) was also among the first to represent a naked Biblical hero. Standing not far away from *David* in Florence is Benvenuto Cellini's bronze nude statue of the mythological Perseus (1545–54) holding up the severed head of Medusa, a work commissioned by Cosimo de' Medici.

Renaissance artists also used nudity for humanistic works displaying ordinary subjects in a realistic manner. This is seen in Dürer's *Naked Hausfrau* (1493) and *Naked Man with Mirror* (*c. 1512*). Later artists followed this trend, with Rembrandt defying classical art with his controversial paintings of fat and elderly nudes, as in *Diana at the Bath* (*c.* 1631) and *Study of a Nude Woman as Cleopatra* (1637), the latter showing an unattractive figure with a snake wrapped around her right leg. Physical ugliness was continued by Georges Rouault (1871–1958), seen in *La Prostituée* (*The Prostitute*) (*c.* 1924–27). Unusually enough, the decrepit nude was also found in sculptures like Auguste Rodin's strangely titled *Celle qui fut la belle Heaulmière* (*She Who Was The Helmet Maker's Once-Beautiful Wife*, 1887).

THIS PUBLIC DISPLAY OF NUDES IN ACTIVE POSES PROVOKED AN OUTCRY FROM RELIGIOUS AND MORAL GROUPS.

The representation of nudity in art became a controversial issue during the Victorian era. Adopting the Renaissance outlook, artists chose classic subjects emphasizing Greek ideals without implying sexuality. They were supported by Queen Victoria and Prince Albert, both of whom were patrons of nude art. Some artists, however, developed the 'sensational nude', such as the statue of *An Athlete Wrestling a Python* (1877) by Frederick, Lord Leighton (1830–96). This public display of nudes in active poses provoked an outcry from religious and moral groups who said they were incitements to vice. Other artists continued to produce nudes of ordinary people. In *Sorrow* (1882) Vincent van Gogh (1853–90) depicted a pregnant woman's grief. Later, Lucian Freud (1922–2011) represented grotesque nudes in works such as *Annabel* (1990) and the obese woman in *Sleeping by the Lion Carpet* (1995–96).

The twentieth century also saw the identity of subjects become lost as nude images turned abstract under the hands of artists like Henri Matisse (1869–1954) and Pablo Picasso (1881–1973), as well as sculptors who included Henry Moore (1898–1986) and Barbara Hepworth (1903–75).

HENRY MOORE

He was born in Castleford, Yorkshire, the seventh of eight children. His father was a coal miner. At the age of 11, he was introduced in Sunday School to Michelangelo's work and decided to become a sculptor.

Moore fought in World War I and was gassed in 1917. He recuperated to become a military instructor. In 1919, he began studying at the Leeds School of Art where he met Barbara Hepworth, who also would go on to sculpt abstract figures, and they became lifelong friends. Moore won a scholarship in 1921 to the Royal College of Art in London and began to produce bronze and stone Surrealist works in which the figures were abstract. 'All art should have a certain mystery and make demands on the spectator,' he later said. 'Everyone thinks that he or she looks [at art], but they don't really, you know'. In 1925, he travelled to Italy to view Renaissance art, an experience that overwhelmed him.

Moore's sculptures feature rounded and swelling shapes that mirror human forms. His series of reclining nudes included *Reclining Figure* (1929) and *Reclining Nude* (1950). He also produced many abstract drawings that he said were made to generate ideas for sculptures, such as *Standing Figures* (1940). He was commissioned as a war artist during World War II and produced a series of drawings of Londoners sheltering in

BELOW: Henry Moore is shown in his studio working on a sculpture commissioned for the Festival of Britain in 1951.

A STUNNING LEGACY

AFTER HENRY MOORE GAINED his diploma in 1924 from the Royal College of Art, the school awarded him a travelling scholarship for six months in Italy to study Renaissance art. The following year, he visited Genoa, Pisa, Assisi and Padua, viewing the works of great artists, and then continued to Rome to see Michelangelo's Sistine Chapel. Moore said experiencing great art had brought him close to a nervous breakdown.

In 1947, he recalled his feelings following the trip: 'For about six months after my return I was never more miserable in my life. Six months exposure to the master works of European art which I saw on my trip had stirred up a violent conflict with my previous ideals. I couldn't seem to shake off the new impressions, or make use of them without denying all that I had devoutly believed in before. I found myself helpless and unable to work'.

underground stations during the Blitz, including *Study for Shelter Sleepers* (1941). His studio was bombed during the war, and he moved to the countryside in Hertfordshire and produced many mother and child works.

From the 1950s, he created outdoor sculptures, such as *Reclining Figure: Festival* for the 1951 Festival of Britain, which sold for £19.1 million in 2012. Others included *Knife-Edge Two-Piece* (1962) for London's Parliament Square and *Reclining Figure* (1969–70) for Columbia University in New York. In his later years, he produced many series of prints, including *Stonehenge* (1972). By the end of the 1970s, his celebrated work was being shown in more than 40 exhibitions each year.

MANNERIST ART

Renaissance painters initiated an art movement of high style known as Mannerism, from the Italian *maniera* meaning 'manner'. This moved away from classical and realistic works to allow artists to create stylistic fantasies. It involved an artiness that combined elegance with the bizarre. Figures were given elongated limbs and placed in contrived poses.

A good example is Parmigianino's *Madonna and Child with Angels* (1534), informally named *Madonna with the Long Neck*. That feature predominates the scene, which also has an oversized infant Jesus in a precarious pose on his mother's lap. Another key example is *An Allegory with Venus and Cupid* (c. 1545) by Bronzino (*b.* Agnolo di Cosimo, 1503–72), an erotic depiction of the two that also includes an hourglass, a howling figure, an old man with wings and a boy stepping on a thorn as he scatters roses. A sculptured work is the Cellini Salt Cellar (1543), a gold-plated salt cellar by Benvenuto Cellini that depicts the reclining figures of Neptune and a nude woman facing each other.

This style lasted from the 1520s until Baroque art began around 1590. The public began to view Mannerism as decadent art, and it declined in popularity until receiving renewed

BELOW: The Cellini Salt Cellar was made for Francis I of France from models that were prepared many years earlier.

interest in the twentieth century, where it was appreciated for its dramatic, experimental style. Some critics now call Mannerism the style that best befits modern creative sensibilities. 'We are mostly Mannerists now,' wrote the art critic Peter Schjeldahl in 2010: 'Art about art, and style for style's sake'. Others have called contemporary art 'postmodern Mannerism'. Another connection is that many viewers during the Renaissance and today expressed disdain for, respectively, Mannerist and 'modern' art.

ABOVE: Parmigianino, who was always fascinated by distortion, painted *Self-portrait in a Convex Mirror* in 1524 when he was 21.

PARMIGIANINO (1503–40)

He was born Girolamo Francesco Maria Mazzola in Parma. He was influenced by Correggio, also from Parma. Between 1522 and 1523, Parmigianino painted frescoes in two chapels of the church of San Giovanni Evangelista in Parma while Correggio painted murals on its dome. In 1524, he went to Rome where three years later he painted *Vision of St Jerome* but was interrupted when soldiers of the Holy Roman Emperor Charles V sacked the city. Parmigianino fled to Bologna, where he painted his masterpiece *Madonna with St Margaret and Other Saints*. He was also a renowned portrait artist whose famous works included that of *Gian Galeazzo Sanvitale* (1524) and of the young woman *Antea* (c. 1535–37)

He developed an influential version of Mannerist art that was elegant with a sensuous beauty that included the distortion and elongation of the human figures. This was also done in the popular etchings he made of his drawings. He returned permanently to Parma in 1531 and in 1534 painted *Madonna and Child with Angels*, also known as *Madonna with the Long*

Neck. He was contracted to paint frescoes on the vault of Santa Maria della Steccata, but he worked so slowly he was imprisoned for breaking his contract.

ARCHITECTURE

The most visible, well-known and reproduced styles of Renaissance architecture are classic triumphant arches and the Doric, Ionic and Corinthian columns, all adopted from the Greek originals. The Renaissance architect who influenced future ones the most was Andrea Palladio. He has also been called the most imitated architect in history. US President Thomas Jefferson (1743–1826), an amateur architect, said in 1816 that Palladio had summed up architecture for all time, describing his *Four Books of Architecture* (1570) as 'the Bible. You should get it and stick close to it'. Palladian architecture was named for him. It became popular between 1715 and 1760 during the Georgian era in Britain and in colonial America. The exteriors were plain and emphasized proportion with Corinthian columns, while interiors were richly decorated.

ANDREA PALLADIO (1508–80)

He was born in Padua, northern Italy, as Andrea di Pietro della Gongola. He moved to nearby Vicenza and at 13 was apprenticed to a stone cutter. He worked as a mason on the villa of the humanist scholar and poet, Gian Giorgio Trissino (1478–1550), who took him on as an assistant and tutored him from 1528 to 1539, renaming him after a character in one of his poems, the guardian angel Palladio.

EARLY COPIES OF ART

ARTISTS WHO DEVELOPED NEW techniques during in the Renaissance quickly saw their influence on contemporaries. They passed on some knowledge to assistants who might be assigned to complete various works. At the same time, there was no way they could protect their new styles that used such innovations as perspective or light and shade. Accusations were made about other artists duplicating their works, producing copies that were hardly distinguishable from the originals.

Albrecht Dürer was infuriated by artistic theft, writing in 1511, 'Beware, you envious thieves of the work and invention of others, keep your thoughtless hands from these works of ours.' He went further, bringing what is believed to be the first case involving art intellectual property law. In Venice, he sued the engraver Marcantonio Raimondi (1480–1534), but the court's panel ruled in favour of Raimondi because he had made small changes from the original.

Trissino took Palladio to Rome in 1541 and 1547, where he observed the ancient ruins. He made his name designing villas for aristocrats. They highlighted classical porticos normally seen in churches, turning them into porches with columns and having rooms laid around. He had decided without proof that since the Pantheon in Rome had a portico, ancient houses probably did.

In 1546, Palladio was commissioned to reconstruct the town hall in Vicenza. Now known as the Basilica, it was not completed until 1617. He returned to live in Rome from 1554 to 1556 where he wrote *Le Antichita de Roma* (*The Antiquities of Rome*), a guide to the city that was used for centuries.

Palladio said he was most influenced by the Roman architect Vitruvius who around 27 BC wrote *De Architectura* (*On Architecture*)

ABOVE: **Villa Godi Malinverni in Veneto, Italy, was built between 1537 and 1542. It was first villa created by Palladio and included a central staircase.**

mostly based on Greek designs. Palladio used Roman architecture to devise rules for design principles of perfect geometry that he believed could be adjusted to any type of building, from the grand to the humble. In 1570, he wrote *I Quattro libri dell'atchitettura* (*Four Books of Architecture*) that summarized the principles of classical architecture. He then concentrated on building several churches in Venice.

The first English architect to be influenced by Palladio was Inigo Jones (1573–1652) in the seventeenth century. A revival of Palladianism then occurred in the eighteenth century following the lavish Baroque style. Palladian buildings are found worldwide, a famous example being the US Capitol Building completed in 1868. The Palladian design is still used following his rules. The Stormont parliamentary building, completed in 1934 in Belfast, Northern Ireland, has a Palladian-styled symmetrical front and central portico. The design remains especially popular in America, seen in Chadsworth College on Figure Eight Island in North Carolina, built in 2005.

SCIENCE

It could be argued that the most important invention during the Renaissance was Gutenberg's printing press with movable type, since this spread the new ideas and art to far regions, in effect keeping the Renaissance alive. As late as the twentieth century, many newspapers and other texts were still composed using individual movable letters, first selected by hand and later using linotype machines operated by a keyboard to set separate hot-metal letters in a line. Today's italic type is also a legacy, first used in 1500 on a page printed by the Venetian printer-publisher Aldus Manutius (1449–1515).

A striking number of Leonardo's inventions or ideas for them were later successfully developed. Using his drawings for a parachute, the British skydiver Adrian Nichols built and successfully flew a version in 2000. 'It took one of the greatest minds who ever lived to design it,' he said, 'but it took 500 years to find a man with a brain small enough to actually go and fly it'. Leonardo's proposal for a submarine became a workable one

BELOW: A replica built in 2002 of Cornelius Van Drebbel's submarine is in the Royal Navy Submarine Museum in Gosport, Hampshire

built in the 1620s by the Danish inventor Cornelius Drebbel, and his plan for an underwater leather diving suit led to scuba gear produced in the 1940s by the French undersea explorers Jacques-Yves Cousteau (1910–97) and Émile Gagnan (1900–79). In 2003, Jacquie Cozens, who produces underwater documentaries, used Leonardo's designs for his version.

LEONARDO'S PURELY MILITARY IDEAS HAVE ALSO PROVED OF VALUE, WITH HIS ARMOURED CAR EVOLVING INTO THE TANK.

Leonardo's purely military ideas have also proved of value, with his armoured car evolving into the tank and his machine gun being refined for the American Civil War. In 1495, he also designed a robotic knight in which a suit of armour was moved by gears on a wheel. This was replicated in 2002 by Mark Rosheim, the NASA robotics designer, using Leonardo's designs.

The ideas of other Renaissance inventors have proven to be credible. The Italian physicist and mathematician Evangelista Torricelli (1608–47) invented a working barometer in 1643 inspired by Galileo's idea, and this is still used today. The modern thermometer, as well, has developed from the thermoscope design of Galileo. His idea was for a tube filled with water and a glass ball that rose and fell with changes in temperature. The Polish-born Dutch physicist Daniel Gabriel Fahrenheit (1686–1736) replaced the water with alcohol in 1704 and then mercury in 1714 to create the modern version. In 1450, Leon Battista Alberti invented the anemometer to measure wind speeds. The device had a disc that would change its angle depending on the force of the wind. This was later refined by Leonardo and

BELOW: Before switching to mercury, Torricelli devised a water barometer 10m (35ft) high, rising above the roof of his house.

later still by the seventeenth-century English scientist Robert Hooke (1635–1703), who also invented a gyroscope for measuring humidity in the air.

MEDICINE

Many believe the ideas of Andreas Vesalius, the Brussels-born professor of Padua University, were the landmarks of modern medicine. He is credited with establishing anatomy

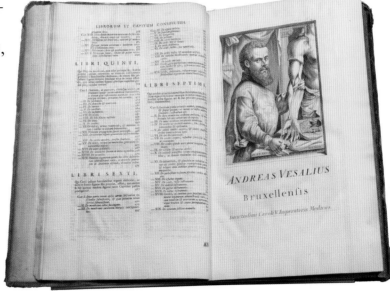

and surgery as practical professional fields. His seven-volume *De Humani Corporis Fabrica* (*The Fabric of the Human Body*), published in 1543, is considered to have created the modern science of anatomy with special insights into cardiovascular anatomy. He taught his students this by having them stand alongside him during dissections. Michelangelo and Leonardo were among artists who used dissections to advance their art, concurrently adding to the knowledge of human anatomy. Several other disciplines have evolved from the works of Renaissance practitioners, such as Paracelsus with toxicology, Girolamo Fracastoro with pathology and Ambroise Paré with forensic pathology. Other physicians struggled with undoing centuries of medical folklore, as did Laurent Joubert whose book *Erreurs Populaires* (*Popular Errors*) caused great controversy in 1577 for its corrections of sexual misinformation.

ABOVE: Vesalius worked with artists to create accurate illustrations for his book on anatomy that made doctors wary of ancient medical practices.

AMBROISE PARÉ (1510–90)

He was born in Bourg-Hersent, France, and in 1533 moved to Paris to become an apprentice to a barber-surgeon, training at Hotel Dieu, a renowned hospital. He was allowed to attend medical lectures at the University of Paris, but they were in Latin, which he did not understand. He joined the army in 1537, and

ABOVE: Pare wrote of war, 'I beseech the great God of victories, that we be never more employed in such misfortune and disaster'.

that same year developed a new method of treating wounds using a soothing balm of turpentine, egg yolk and rose oil, replacing the painful, cauterizing boiling oil that had hitherto been employed. He also forewent hot irons to stop haemorrhaging during amputations in favour of ligatures.

In 1545, he studied anatomy in Paris and in 1552 became surgeon to King Henry II (*r.* 1547–59). He would continue to hold this position for successive French kings for the remainder of his life, serving Francis II (1559–60), Charles IX (1560–74) and Henry III (1574–89).

Paré's methods were intended to replace a patient's extreme pain during operations (accepted then as necessary) with a gentle treatment that would be to their overall betterment. He was the first barber-surgeon to write in French instead of Latin and the first to record his procedures. His writings spread the new idea of healing the body with the least suffering to the patient and the least damage to his tissues. He improved ways to implant teeth and artificial limbs and invented artificial eyes made from enamelled glass, gold, silver and porcelain.

Paré served as a military surgeon for 30 years before becoming a surgeon in Paris, where he cared for the sick and the poor. In 1575, he published *Les Oeuvres*, a collection of his writings. He has been called the father of modern surgery and forensic pathology. 'There are five duties of surgery', he wrote, 'to remove what is superfluous, to restore what has been dislocated, to separate what has grown together, to reunite what has been divided and to redress the defects of nature.'

LAURENT JOUBERT (1529–82)
He was the tenth of 20 children born in the province of Dauphiné in south-central France. At the age of 21, Joubert

studied medicine at the University of Montpellier under the renowned anatomist Guillaume Rondelet (1507–66), receiving his doctorate in 1558. After Rondelet's death, Joubert became chancellor of the Faculty of Medicine at the request of students. Catherine de Medici then appointed him as her physician, and he later became physician to three French kings.

Joubert wrote several medical books in French and Latin. The most influential and controversial was *Erreurs Populaires* (*Popular Errors*) published in 1577, the first of 19 editions, written for lay readers to correct popular misconceptions and prejudices. Among those was the belief that boys were born during a full moon and girls during a new one. He also disputed the idea that a woman in labour should keep her husband's hat on her stomach, and he unusually recommended that a woman should stand at the moment of birth since the child's weight would aid its delivery. The most shocking advice concerned female sexuality, such as his denial that infertility could be cured by sexual relations during a woman's monthly period because conception was then impossible 'and this is why one [should] abstain from such nastiness'. Despite charges of indecency, the book earned Joubert respect for his knowledge of conception and pregnancy, with Henry III calling him to Paris to discuss his queen's infertility.

Joubert died on 21 October 1582, supposedly while travelling on a stormy night to see a patient in a village near Montpellier.

BELOW: Joubert's *Erreurs Populaires* also dealt with sleep, air, appetite and proper food. He originally planned to write 30 volumes.

ABOVE: This image of Vespucci meeting an allegorical representation of the New World was painted in the late 1580s by Giovanni Stradano.

EXPLORATION

The audacious voyages of Renaissance explorers opened up new worlds to Europeans who were able to swap products, cultures and information with the natives, a process that became known as the Columbian Exchange. The geography of the world was never the same after the Age of Exploration and Discovery that was driven by Columbus, Magellan, Cook, Drake, Vespucci, Dias, Cortez, Pizarro, Cabot, Vasco da Gama and many others. Their bold journeys into the unknown created settlements, colonies and new nations but also subjection, slavery and disease. Competition for new lands inevitably led to wars that redrew world maps many times, as seen in the changing size of the British Empire.

Future explorers were the beneficiaries of the knowledge gathered by those who first crossed the open seas. New navigational aids such as the magnetic compass were developed as well as navigational charts. The experiences of long voyages were handed down, from the type of ship required to the selection and storage of foods.

WILLEM JANSZOON (1570-1630)

He captained a ship of the Dutch East India Company during the competition in the early seventeenth century with the Portuguese, Spanish and English for control of the East Indies (now Indonesia). Despite this, Janszoon (also known as Jansz) from Amsterdam was an explorer who found time in 1606 to become the first European to discover Australia and map its northern coast.

Janszoon's ship was the *Duyfen* ('Little Dove') sent in 1605 to find New Guinea, which supposedly had large deposits of gold. After sailing along the western coast of New Guinea, he continued until touching down on the coast of Australia's future Queensland. This contact on 26 February 1606 is the first recorded landfall of a European on the Australian continent.

BELOW: An early map of New Holland (now Australia) and New Zealand based on information from seventeenth-century Dutch explorers.

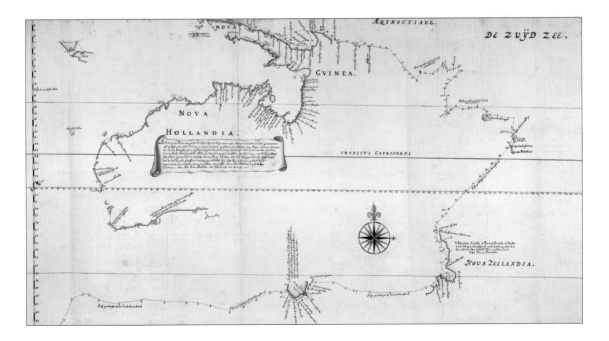

During land expeditions, ten of his crew were killed by natives. He then charted about 320km (199 miles) of the coastline believing it was an extension of New Guinea. He repeated this mistake after returning to the Netherlands in 1611, and Dutch maps retained the error for many years. Nevertheless, future navigators referred to his coastal map. A more accurate one would be drawn only a century later by Britain's James Cook (1728–79).

CANNONS ON WARSHIPS

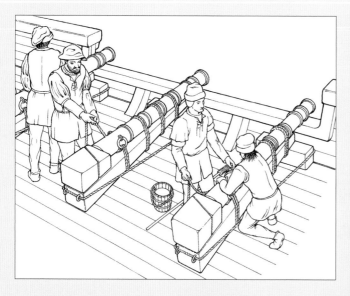

Cannons could cause danger to a ship's crew. As they became heavier, they were put on lower decks and fired through gunports.

NAVAL WARFARE WAS CHANGED for centuries when cannons were introduced on warships during the Renaissance. Their first recorded use was in 1338 at the Battle of Arnemuiden, the first naval engagement of the Hundred Years' War between England and France. The English ship *Christofer* (also spelt *Christopher*) carried three cannons. Despite this admittedly small artillery, the English fleet was the loser.

As more warships were armed, naval battles no longer depended on ramming and boarding vessels. An attacker could fire from a distance to sink the enemy and even shoot at land targets. Cannons on ships were even better situated than those on land, as they were much easier to float to battle than haul over rough terrain and in bad weather. A disadvantage was the recoil when fired. This was solved by placing them on wheels and tying them to the deck. The other problem was the danger of flying splinters caused by an incoming cannonball. A ship's firepower was increased in the late fifteenth century when rifles were introduced. It was a marksman who shot and killed Admiral Lord Nelson at the Battle of Trafalgar in 1805, in which the largest ships carried 100 cannons.

Janszoon was made an admiral in the Dutch Navy and in 1619 captured four ships of the British East India Company, for which he was decorated with a chain of honour. In 1629, he was admiral of a fleet whose seven ships carried out a diplomatic visit to India.

LITERATURE

The legacy of Renaissance literature is that much of it has never died. Today's readers enjoy the insights, wisdom and wit of extraordinary writers like Dante, Chaucer, Cervantes and Shakespeare, with the latter's plays also regularly staged and filmed. Many Renaissance authors are studied and discussed in university classes, perpetuating their views on the human condition and life's serious choices, such as religion, philosophy and politics. Virtually any Renaissance idea is available to today's seeker with all texts available in the vernacular languages that displaced Latin.

Shakespeare, as well, generated themes, storylines and plot devices still used by modern authors. Three books that took their titles from Shakespearean lines, include: *Brave New World* by Aldous Huxley, from *the Tempest*, and there are several references to the Bard in the story; *The Dogs of War* by Frederick Forsyth, from *Julius Caesar*; and *Cakes and Ale* by W. Somerset Maugham from *Twelfth Night*.

Shakespeare also created more than 17,000 words and phrases still in our language. Words include: bedazzled, dauntless, dwindle, lacklustre, swindle, unearthly and unreal. Among phrases are: break the ice, jealousy is the green-eyed monster, melted into thin air, flesh and blood, send him packing, too much of a good thing and the world is my oyster.

ABOVE: The authors Huxley, Forsyth and Maugham were among the many writers who have been influenced by the brilliance of Shakespeare.

JOHN DONNE (1572–1631)

Modern poets have expressed special admiration for Donne. His popularity declined after the Restoration but had a remarkable

revival in the nineteenth century when the English poets Samuel
Taylor Coleridge (1772–1834) and later Robert Browning (1812
–89) voiced their enthusiasm for his works. More admiration
followed from twentieth-century poets like T.S. Eliot (1888–
1965), who praised him as a proto-modernist, and William
Butler Yeats (1865–1939).

Donne influenced later poets by his very personal style and
with casual rhythms of speech, a great innovation in his time.
This is seen in the line 'For God's sake hold your tongue, and
let me love' in 'The Canonization'. He also wrote poems about
ordinary subjects, such as 'The Flea'. He is considered to be an
early metaphysical writer who used irony and a cynical tone

when needed. Donne has been called the greatest love poet in the English language. He gave his subjects a contemporary look, as seen in 'The Good-Morrow' when two lovers reference the Age of Exploration:

'Let sea-discoverers to new worlds have gone,
Let maps to others, worlds on worlds have shown,
Let us possess one world, each hath one, and is one.'

Donne was born in London and studied at Oxford and Cambridge universities without taking a degree. In 1592, he read law at Lincoln's Inn in London. In 1597, he sailed with Sir Walter Raleigh to the Azores and returned that year to become secretary to the Attorney General Sir Thomas Egerton (1540–1617). He caused a scandal in 1601 by secretly marrying Anne More, the niece of Lady Egerton. He was dismissed and briefly imprisoned, forcing the couple to live in poverty for years. Donne, a Roman Catholic, was ordained in the Church of England in 1615 and became chaplain to King James I. He was known as an emotional and powerful preacher, and in 1621 was made Dean of St Paul's Cathedral in London. He continued preaching and writing for a decade until his death. Almost none of his poetry had been published during his lifetime, although *Anniversaries* was published between 1611 and 1612. Two editions of his poems were posthumously published in 1633 and 1635.

MUSIC

Renaissance humanism played the leading role in the evolution of modern music. The domination of religious music gave way to the classic idea of music as expressive art with the power to move human passions. A leading advocate was the Italian humanist Marsilio Ficino (1433–99)

BELOW: Ficino was also a philosopher and priest. 'Never worry about anything', he said. 'Live in the present. Live now. Be happy'.

Interpres divi vigilans, Ficine, Platonis,
Ingenio est illi lux data quanta tuo.

who believed in the close relationship of music and the spiritual. He said singing was a 'contemplation of the divine', believing music could attract the spiritual influence of a planet's rays. He revived Plato's *musica humana*, human music, in terms of *animae musica*, music of the soul.

Drama and emotion also popularized the madrigal that was introduced in Italy in the 1520s. The Flemish composer Cipriano de Rore (*c.* 1515–65) moved to Italy and emphasized intensity of expression for the form, interpreting well-known poems through his music. Among the many moods he created were the drama of changing weather and the lively interplay of various voices.

The most visible legacy of Renaissance music is the violin, introduced in the middle of the sixteenth century. The first recorded makers of the instrument were from northern Italy: Andrea Amati from Cremona and Gasparo di Bertolotti (1542–1609). Some of their instruments still exist, including the world's oldest known violin, crafted by Amati in about 1564.

THE AMATI FAMILY

Andrea Amati (*c.*1520–78) created the first violin, an instrument whose style would be refined by his sons into the modern instrument. He was born in Cremona, Italy, and around 1546 made his earliest-known violin. The oldest surviving one is from 1564. His choice of varnish with an amber colour is still used today. His fame spread and France's King Charles IX (*r.* 1560–74) ordered 38 instruments that included violins of two sizes, violas and large cellos. Surviving instruments from that collection bear the king's coat of arms.

When Amati first worked on his violin, instruments resembling primitive violins had three strings. He added a fourth that could be tuned to produce notes that are perfect fifths.

His sons, Antonio (*c.*1550–1638) and Girolamo (1551–1635) worked together, continuing to produce outstanding violins. Girolamo's son, Nicola (1596–1684) became known for fashioning violin masterpieces. He also taught the craft to Antonio Stradivari also from Cremona, who would raise violin-

Amati's
lin made
arles IX,
shmolean
ford,

making to perfection. Another of Nicola's students, learning with Stradivari, was Andrea Guarneri (c. 1626–98) who produced another famous violin-making family in Cremona.

ANTONIO STRADIVARI (*c.* 1644–1737)

While still a student in Nicola Amati's workshop, Stradivari (Stradivarius in Latin) began to fashion his own small violins in 1666 and put his own labels on them. By 1684, he made larger models. He experimented to improve the proportions, creating the instrument's modern bridge, also fashioning a flat and shallow body that produces a lovely soprano tone, and in 1690 crafted longer versions. These experiments resulted in acoustically perfect violins. Some attribute this partly to his use of a secret varnish whose formula has never been revealed or discovered. What is known is that Stradivari gave uncompromising attention to details and materials, like the maple wood he used treated with chemicals.

The 'Strad' became so commercially successful, his contemporaries coined the phrase 'rich as Stradivari'. From 1714–1716, his workshop annually produced an average of 16 violins. He also made violas, cellos, guitars and harps. It is estimated he produced more than 1100 instruments, of which some 650 still survive. Stradivari violins today sell for millions at auction.

Stradivari died at the age of 93. His sons Francesco (1671–1743) and Omobono (1679–1742), who had worked with him, were then in their 60s and retired.

POLITICS

Humanism was a major reason the politics of the Renaissance moved away from religious and authoritarian rule. People became weary of wars between popes and monarchs, or popes against popes, or monarchs against monarchs. The time had come for city states to reject the authority of the pope and emperor in favour of popular sovereignty and active citizenship. The transition would be bumpy, having to survive France's invasion of Italy and the Italian Wars as well as the

BELOW: Stradivari's 'Regent' violin was produced in 1708 and is still played, having developed an even richer tone in 300 years.

political pessimism of Machiavelli and others. New democratic systems could turn out to be corrupt illusions. Nevertheless, citizens eventually developed political processes to keep elite families from ruling. The small size of city states made it easier for citizens to influence their government, by taking part in an assembly or council, for example. Most governments were actually oligarchies ruled by the few. In Venice in the fourteenth century, only members of some 200 patrician families could belong to the Great Council from among a population of 120,000. Trade guilds eventually became powerful enough to demand that government by the elite be transferred to them, and in some city states one had to be a guild member to run for political office.

Humanist political thought was on an inexorable path towards representative government and individual liberty. All five Italian city states were republics of some form, all considering themselves heirs of Greek and Roman republics. One strong voice promoting this was Michel de Montaigne, the French writer and philosopher who wrote constantly about the independence and freedom of the self.

The Renaissance also developed a form of modern diplomacy when city states established permanent embassies in foreign courts, an innovation that spread to European countries such as France and England.

MICHEL DE MONTAIGNE (1533–92)

He was born Michel Eyquem de Montaigne at the Chateau Montaigne 48km (30 miles) from Bordeaux, France, into a rich family that had profited from commerce. His father was mayor of Bordeaux. He was first educated by a German tutor then studied at the College of Guyenne under the

Scottish humanist George Buchanan (1506–82). Michel studied law at the University of Toulouse and in 1557 served in the Parliament of Bordeaux. In 1570 he sold his parliamentary seat and retired the next year to the castle of Montaigne where he had been born. From 1571 to 1580, he wrote two books of *Essais* (*Attempts*) published in 1580. He then travelled for 15 months to Germany, Switzerland, Austria and Italy. While travelling, he was elected as mayor of Bordeaux and served from 1581 to 1585. He completed his third book of *Essais* in 1587 and while visiting Paris that year was arrested and imprisoned by the Protestant League because of his support for Catholic Henry III. While in Paris, he published his fifth book of *Essais*.

BESIDES REJECTING THE RULE OF THE ROMAN CATHOLIC CHURCH, CITIZENS WERE FACED WITH A DECISION ABOUT PROTESTANTISM.

His *Essais*, which gave the name to the English 'essay', were written during religious conflicts and persecutions in France between Catholics and Protestants. His books promote the individual self, although imperfect and ever-changing, as the only entity that can search for truth and not from other imposed ideas. 'I am myself the matter of my book', he wrote. Yet he emphasized keeping contact with others and upholding freedom. He supported the value of independent judgement over blindly accepting the opinions of others.

Those who expressed admiration for Montaigne's work included the American essayist and poet Ralph Waldo Emerson (1803–82) and the German classical scholar and philosopher Friedrich Nietzsche (1844–1900).

RELIGION

Besides rejecting the rule of the Roman Catholic Church, citizens were faced with a decision about Protestantism. The Protestant Reformation brought comfort to those who could not accept Catholic doctrine, but also the pain of religious prejudice and persecution, which happened after Henry VIII broke with the Vatican. Even today, a Catholic cannot be king or queen of the United Kingdom, since the monarch is also head of the Protestant Church of England.

FOLLOWING PAGE:

The tragedy of the St Bartolomew's Day Massacre was painted in 1572 by the French Huguenot artist Francois Dubois.

ABOVE: Billy Graham preached to about 40,000 people on 27 October 1957 at the Polo Grounds in New York City.

Violence on the streets was an element in the rise of Protestantism, as seen in 1572 in the St Bartholomew's Day massacre of Protestant Huguenots by Catholics in Paris. That legacy has continued into the modern era, as in Northern Ireland where supporters of the two religions have clashed and affected politics.

The United States, as well, has experienced the political power of religion. Before the charismatic John F. Kennedy stood for president in 1960, the two major political parties had only selected one Catholic candidate, Al Smith in 1928, who lost disastrously. Opponents warned he would take directions from the pope. None since has been chosen. Protestant television evangelists have also urged followers to make certain political choices, a prime example being Jerry Falwell, a conservative activist who formed the Moral Majority in 1979 and who has been credited by some with helping elect President Ronald Reagan in 1980.

Despite today's lingering prejudices, the Protestant Reformation that Luther inaugurated during the Renaissance has resulted in some 33,000 Protestant denominations that exist peacefully with Catholic churches. The appeal of Protestantism so evident during the Renaissance has endured, as seen in the success of the American evangelist Billy Graham who, at his height from the 1940s onwards, preached to nearly 215 million people in 185 countries and territories.

VATICAN II

In a belated response to humanism and Protestantism, the Roman Catholic Church made significant changes during its Second Vatican Council, commonly called Vatican II, from 1962 to 1965. Called by Pope John XXIII (r. 1958–63), it was the first ecumenical council to review doctrinal issues in nearly a century. Meeting at St Peter's Basilica in Rome, the bishops approved 16 documents that would help the Church engage with the modern world, the first change in its defensive inflexibility since the Protestant Reformation.

BELOW: Bishops are shown entering St Peter's on 11 October 1962 for Vatican II. Also participating were cardinals and other church dignitaries.

For the first time, vernacular languages could be used during the Mass. Catholics could pray with Christians from other denominations because they shared a common belief in God, reversing the understanding that they should not worship in non-Catholic churches. The priest would now face the congregation instead of showing his back, a change to show worshippers they were an important part of the service. Jews would no longer be stigmatized for killing Christ but be seen as having a covenant with God; the Church also acknowledged its Jewish roots.

JERRY FALWELL (1933–2007)

He was born in Lynchburg, Virginia, USA, as Jerry Laymon Falwell, the son of an atheist. He said he 'accepted Jesus Christ' at the age of 18. He studied at Lynchburg College and then Baptist Bible College in Springfield, Missouri, graduating in 1956. Falwell returned to Lynchburg that year to establish the Thomas Road Baptist Church with 35 members and broadcast his sermons on the *Old-Time Gospel Hour* on radio and television. In 1971, he founded and headed Liberty Bible College (later Liberty University) in Lynchburg. He followed a fundamental conservative Protestant faith and condemned such 'godless' activities as gay rights, abortion and feminism but did renounce his early support of segregation.

Falwell's political activism led him to establish the Moral Majority in 1979 as a conservative political lobbying organization that he said was 'pro-life, pro-traditional family, pro-moral, pro-American and pro-Israel'. He said the way to build membership was to 'Get them saved, baptized and registered'. It helped create the religious right as a political force. Its membership grew to several million and seemed to be a force in President Reagan's election. Falwell disbanded it in 1989 saying it had accomplished its mission. Among his books in the 1980s were *Listen America* (1980), *The Fundamentalist Phenomenon* (1981) and *Champions for God* (1985).

Falwell continued to support the Republican Party and was a harsh critic of the Democrats and President Bill Clinton. In 2004, he founded the Faith and Values Coalition (later the Moral

Majority Coalition). When he died, his Lynchburg church had grown from 35 members to more than 20,000, and he claimed his international television programme was seen by more than 50 million regular viewers.

ABOVE: Falwell's political, social and religious messages were hard to separate and appealed to his large audience of conservatives.

THE LEGACY CONTINUES

The influence of the Renaissance continues to the present day, a legacy that is both abiding and complex. It can easily be seen in the grand Palladium buildings around the world but more often is the subtle influence behind the work of artists, writers, musicians, philosophers, doctors, scientists, politicians and the clergy. Of special relevance, it has given people a new humanist way of thinking, the ability to make important decisions that were previously made by others.

BIBLIOGRAPHY

Anderson, Christy, *Renaissance Architecture* (Oxford University Press, 2013)

Armstrong, Carol M.; Bailey, Colin B., *Manet: Portraying Life* (Royal Academy of Arts, 2013)

Aston, Margaret (Ed.), *Renaissance Complete* (Thames & Hudson, 2009)

Atlas, Alan W., *Renaissance Music* (W. W. Norton, 1998)

Bergreen, Laurence, *Columbus: The Four Voyages, 1492-1504* (Penguin, 2013)

Burckhardt, Jacob, *The Civilization of the Renaissance in Italy* (Penguin Classics, 1990)

Campbell, Gordon (Ed.), *The Oxford Illustrated History of the Renaissance* (Oxford University Press, 2019)

Campbell, Stephen J., *A New History of Italian Renaissance Art* (Thames & Hudson, 2017)

Celenza, Christopher S., *Petrarch: Everywhere a Wanderer* (Reaktion Books, 2017)

Chapman, Alan, *Stargazers: Copernius, Galileo, the Telescope and the Church* (Lion Books, 2014)

Cliff, Nigel, *The Last Crusade: The Epic Voyages of Vasco da Gama* (Atlantic Books, 2013)

Comerford, Brendan, *The Pilgrim's Story: The Life and Spirituality of St. Ignatius Loyola* (Messenger Publications, 2017)

Crowley, Roger, *Conquerors: How Portugal Forged the First Global Empire* (Faber & Faber, 2016)

Crowley, Roger, *Constantinople: The Last Great Siege, 1453* (Faber & Faber, 2013)

Davis, Robert C.; Lindsmith, Beth, *Renaissance People: Lives that Shaped the Modern Age* (Thames & Hudson, 2019)

Eclercy, Bastian, *Titian and the Renaissance in Venice* (Prestel Publishing, 2019)

Eire, Carlos M. N., *Reformations: The Early Modern World, 1450-1650* (Yale University Press, 2016)

Faber, Toby, *Stradivari's Genius* (Random House Trade, 2006)

Field, J. V., *The Invention of Infinity: Mathematics and Art in the Renaissance* (Oxford University Press, 1997)

Fudge, Thomas A., *The Trial of Jan Hus* (Oxford University Press, 2013)

Gamberini, Andrea, *The Italian Renaissance State* (Cambridge University Press, 2014)

Goldthwaite, Richard A., *The Economy of Renaissance Florence* (Johns Hopkins University Press, 2011)

Gray, Hanna Holborn, *Renaissance Humanism* (Bobbs-Merrill, 1963)

Greenstein, Jack M., *The Creation of Eve and Renaissance Naturalism* (Cambridge University Press, 2016)

Hibbert, Christopher, *The Rise and Fall of the House of Medici* (Penguin, 1979)

Holmes, George, *Art and Politics in Renaissance Italy* (Oxford University Press/British Academy, 1995)

Isaacson, Walter, *Leonardo da Vinci* (Simon & Schuster, 2018)

Lahey, Stephen Edmund, *John Wyclif* (Oxford University Press, 2008)

Man, John, *The Gutenberg Revolution* (Bantam, 2009)

Metaxas, Eric, *Martin Luther* (Viking Press, 2017)

Nethersole, Scott, *Art in Renaissance Florence: A City and its Legacy* (Laurence King, 2019)

O'Malley, John W., *What Happened at Vatican II* (Harvard University Press, 2010)

Porras, Stephanie, *Art of the Northern Renaissance: Courts, Commerce and Devotion* (Laurence King, 2018)

Richmond, Robin, *Michelangelo and the Creation of the Sistine Chapel* (Random House, 2001)

Riggs, David, *The World of Christopher Marlowe* (Faber & Faber, 2005)

Sawday, Jonathan, *The Body Embrazoned: Dissection and the Human Body in Renaissance Culture* (Routledge, 1996)

Smith, Emma, *This is Shakespeare* (Pelican Books, 2019)

Vanhoutte, Jacqueline, *Age in Love: Shakespeare and the Elizabethan Court* (University of Nebraska Press, 2019)

Welch, Evelyn, *Art in Renaissance Italy, 1350-1500* (Oxford University Press, 2000)

Wolf, Norbert, *Albrecht Durer* (Prestel, 2017)

INDEX

Page numbers in *italic* refer to
illustration captions

PICTURE CREDITS